Microwave Magic
Brunch

 Grolier Limited
TORONTO

Contributors to this series:

Recipes and Technical Assistance:
École de cuisine Bachand-Bissonnette
Cooking consultants:
Denis Bissonette
Michèle Émond
Dietician:
Christiane Barbeau
Photos:
Laramée Morel Communications
Audio-Visuelles
Design:
Claudette Taillefer
Assistants:
Julie Deslauriers
Philippe O'Connor
Joan Pothier
Accessories:
Andrée Cournoyer
Writing:
Communications La Griffe Inc.
Text Consultants:
Cap et bc inc.
Advisors:
Roger Aubin
Joseph R. De Varennes
Gaston Lavoie
Kenneth H. Pearson

Assembly:
Carole Garon
Vital Lapalme
Jean-Pierre Larose
Carl Simmons
Gus Soriano
Marc Vallières
Production Managers:
Gilles Chamberland
Ernest Homewood
Production Assistants:
Martine Gingras
Catherine Gordon
Kathy Kishimoto
Peter Thomlison
Art Director:
Bernard Lamy
Editors:
Laurielle Ilacqua
Susan Marshall
Margaret Oliver
Robin Rivers
Lois Rock
Jocelyn Smyth
Donna Thomson
Dolores Williams
Development:
Le Groupe Polygone Éditeurs Inc.

We wish to thank the following firms, PIER I IMPORTS and LE CACHE POT, for their contribution to the illustration of this set.

The series editors have taken every care to ensure that the information given is accurate. However, no cookbook can guarantee the user successful results. The editors cannot accept any responsibility for the results obtained by following the recipes and recommendations given.

Canadian Cataloguing in Publication Data

Main entry under title:

Brunch

(Microwave magic ; 23)
Translation of: Le Brunch.
Includes index.
ISBN 0-7172-2444-9

1. Microwave cookery.   2. Brunches.
I. Series: Microwave magic (Toronto, Ont.) ; 23.

TX832.B7813 1988   641.5'882   C88-094222-3

Contents

Microwave Magic is a multi-volume set, with each volume devoted to a particular type of cooking. So, if you are looking for a chicken recipe, you simply go to one of the two volumes that deal with poultry. Each volume has its own index, and the final volume contains a general index to the complete set.

Microwave Magic puts over twelve hundred recipes at your fingertips. You will find it as useful as the microwave oven itself. Enjoy!

Note from the Editor

How to Use this Book
The books in this set have been designed to make your job as easy as possible. As a result, most of the recipes are set out in a standard way.

We suggest that you begin by consulting the information chart for the recipe you have chosen. You will find there all the information you need to decide if you are able to make it: preparation time, cost per serving, level of difficulty, number of calories per serving and other relevant details. Thus, if you have only 30 minutes in which to prepare the evening meal, you will quickly be able to tell which recipe is possible and suits your schedule.

The list of ingredients is always clearly separated from the main text. When space allows, the ingredients are shown together in a photograph so that you can make sure you have them all without rereading the list—

another way of saving your valuable time. In addition, for the more complex recipes we have supplied photographs of the key stages involved either in preparation or serving.

All the dishes in this book have been cooked in a 700 watt microwave oven. If your oven has a different wattage, consult the conversion chart that appears on the following page for cooking times in different types of oven. We would like to emphasize that the cooking times given in the book are a minimum. If a dish does not seem to be cooked enough, you may return it to the oven for a few more minutes. Also, the cooking time can vary according to your ingredients: their water and fat content, thickness, shape and even where they come from. We have therefore left a blank space on each recipe page in which you can note

the cooking time that suits you best. This will enable you to add a personal touch to the recipes that we suggest and to reproduce your best results every time.

Although we have put all the technical information together at the front of this book, we have inserted a number of boxed entries called **MICROTIPS** throughout to explain particular techniques. They are brief and simple, and will help you obtain successful results in your cooking.

With the very first recipe you try, you will discover just how simple microwave cooking can be and how often it depends on techniques you already use for cooking with a conventional oven. If cooking is a pleasure for you, as it is for us, it will be all the more so with a microwave oven. Now let's get on with the food.

The Editor

Key to the Symbols
For ease of reference, the following symbols have been used on the recipe information charts.

The pencil symbol ✏️ is a reminder to write your cooking time in the space provided.

Level of Difficulty

🍴 Easy

🍴🍴 Moderate

🍴🍴🍴 Complex

Cost per Serving

$ Inexpensive

$ $ Moderate

$ $ $ Expensive

Power Levels

All the recipes in this book have been tested in a 700 watt oven. As there are many microwave ovens on the market with different power levels, and as the names of these levels vary from one manufacturer to another, we have decided to give power levels as a percentage. To adapt the power levels given here, consult the chart opposite and the instruction manual for your oven.

Generally speaking, if you have a 500 watt or 600 watt oven you should increase cooking times by about 30% over those given, depending on the actual length of time required. The shorter the original cooking time, the greater the percentage by which it must be lengthened. The 30% figure is only an average. Consult the chart for detailed information on this topic.

Power Levels

HIGH: 100% - 90%	Vegetables (except boiled potatoes and carrots) Soup Sauce Fruits Browning ground beef Browning dish Popcorn
MEDIUM HIGH: 80% - 70%	Rapid defrosting of precooked dishes Muffins Some cakes Hot dogs
MEDIUM: 60% - 50%	Cooking tender meat Cakes Fish Seafood Eggs Reheating Boiled potatoes and carrots
MEDIUM LOW: 40%	Cooking less tender meat Simmering Melting chocolate
DEFROST: 30% **LOW: 30% - 20%**	Defrosting Simmering Cooking less tender meat
WARM: 10%	Keeping food warm Allowing yeast dough to rise

Cooking Time Conversion Chart

700 watts	600 watts*
5 s	11 s
15 s	20 s
30 s	40 s
45 s	1 min
1 min	1 min 20 s
2 min	2 min 40 s
3 min	4 min
4 min	5 min 20 s
5 min	6 min 40 s
6 min	8 min
7 min	9 min 20 s
8 min	10 min 40 s
9 min	12 min
10 min	13 min 30 s
20 min	26 min 40 s
30 min	40 min
40 min	53 min 40 s
50 min	66 min 40 s
1 h	1 h 20 min

* There is very little difference in cooking times between 500 watt ovens and 600 watt ovens.

Brunch: The Perfect Opportunity to Combine Elegance and Informality

Brunch—the word itself is a relatively recent coinage and a typically North American one. As everyone knows, it contracts and combines the words *breakfast* and *lunch* for a true representation of the meal it designates.

While the word may be fairly new, however, the custom that gave it birth is an ancient one. Similarly, while the word itself may be North American, the practice of eating a more copious first meal of the day on those rare occasions when time allows—and eating it rather later than usual—is virtually universal. The proof, if one is needed, is that the word is now used around the world and has been adopted into a number of other languages.

More often than not, the word—in any language—has come to mean something more than just a combined breakfast and lunch for whoever happens to be around. Usually when we use it we are talking about a casual but nonetheless carefully planned meal to which one or more guests are invited. It may begin anytime between ten o'clock and noon, but an essential characteristic is the relaxed, leisurely pace at which it is served. (Brunches have been known to stretch on to mid-afternoon—or even longer.)

A brunch menu can be simplicity itself—a couple of uncomplicated dishes accompanied by a good cup of coffee—or it can be very elaborate with one succulent creation followed by another even more exquisite.

Usually, a brunch menu is something of a hybrid, partaking of the nature of both breakfast and lunch. Like a good substantial breakfast, it will usually include fruit and fruit juices, jams, preserves and a selection of breads and rolls, cheeses, yoghurt and coffee. Without becoming a complete buffet, it may well include several lunch or dinner items: salads, raw or cooked vegetables, hot or cold meat and seafood dishes, a selection of desserts, light wines and punches. The very essence of a brunch is its unconventional, eclectic nature.

But the particularly wide range of menu possibilities is not the only distinctive feature of a brunch. The occasion carries with it an atmosphere of relaxed gaiety, and even a hint of self-indulgence is not out of place. Moreover, no other meal adapts itself more readily to the changing seasons. Build your menu around items that are in season and serve it outside on the patio in summer, or around the fire in your coziest room in winter.

Any festive occasion—Mother's Day, Easter, Christmas, a birthday—can provide the excuse for a brunch. But really, why wait for an excuse? A bit of advance planning and a yen for the companionship of friends and family are all you need.

Planning Your Brunch

A successful brunch is one where both you and your guests can devote yourselves to the leisurely enjoyment of good food in a relaxed atmosphere. This does not necessarily mean that you must spend hours and hours preparing a vast array of dishes ahead of time. It does, however, require that you do some careful advance planning, taking into consideration the amount of time, effort and money you are prepared to put into it. In the end, a brunch is no more difficult to plan than your family's weekly meals. A surprisingly few well-chosen additions to your shopping list will break the monotony of everyday menus and allow you to impress and delight your guests.

Step One: Establishing a Menu

In the case of a brunch—as indeed of most things—good planning is a matter of common sense, technique and experience.

The first, and very important, step is to establish your menu —that is, to choose precisely what dishes you will serve and in what order—so that you avoid finding yourself obliged to improvise. There are a number of questions that you should ask yourself at this point: Will your brunch be served at the dining table or more casually in the family room? Or is the weather likely to be ideal for an outdoor brunch? Does the particular time of year have some special treat to offer? Who are your guests and what do you know about their individual preferences? Do you want to serve the meal yourself or set as much as possible out in advance so that you can spend more time sitting with your guests? How much do you want to spend on the brunch? Will you have any help? Do the dishes that you are thinking of complement one another? What can you do to make your table and the food you are serving as attractive as possible? Answering questions such as these at this stage will save you a lot of worries later.

It goes without saying that a brunch served by the fire as a pale winter light filters in through frost-covered windows will be quite different from one served out in the shade of an old maple tree whose leaves are being gently stirred by a light summer breeze. The former will probably include a number of hearty and comforting hot dishes, whereas the latter will tend to put the emphasis on light, refreshing food and cool drinks.

Even the equipment you require will change with the seasons. A cooler, for instance, can save you a lot of running back and forth between your kitchen and your patio during an outdoor brunch, but it would obviously serve no purpose whatsoever if your brunch is being served three steps away from your refrigerator.

No matter what the time of year, your brunch will have that extra touch of class if you remember to include seasonable items—fresh fruit or vegetables, certain shellfish, meats, wines—that are available only at this particular time.

Since your object, naturally, is to please your guests, you will want to give some thought to their particular tastes. Often the simple addition of a particular condiment, spice or relish is all it takes to ensure a guest's enjoyment.

You cannot, of course, cater to everyone's every preference, and you should therefore try to achieve a pleasant balance among the dishes you are serving. Make sure that there is sufficient variety and that all dishes are served in sufficient quantity so that guests can—and will want to—try everything.

Do remember, however, that a brunch is not a formal dinner. Certainly, it can be copious, but it can also be a light and fairly simple meal, tastefully presented. To some extent, the amount of money you are prepared to spend will affect the style of the brunch you decide to serve. Remember to keep this in mind as you choose your menu.

The amount of time you feel you can put into preparation is equally important. If you have plenty of time and enjoy shopping and cooking, you can allow yourself to choose exotic and out-of-the-ordinary items that will require extra time to find and prepare. If, on the other hand, you have little time (and/or inclination) to devote to shopping and preparation, you should restrict your menu to readily available items that are quickly prepared and cooked. The fact that you will—or will not—have help with all the various chores involved in preparing and serving your brunch is something you should take into consideration.

More than any other meal perhaps, a brunch, by its very nature, calls for an element of the fanciful. This can be expressed not only in the taste of the food you serve but also in its appearance and that of your table. Give some thought to decorative touches that you can add and to whether the dishes you have chosen will create appealing color combinations. If a special occasion is the reason (or excuse) for your brunch, it may well suggest its own particular colors and shapes that you may wish to play up.

As you can see, there are many things to think about and now, several days ahead, is the time to think about them. We would also advise that you not settle your menu definitively when you first sit down to plan it. Draft it and then look it over the next day. The best ideas often need some time to mature.

Step Two: Making a Shopping List

The second, equally important step in planning a brunch consists of making as complete and precise a list as possible of the items you have to buy and the quantities of each that you need. This can be easily prepared from the lists of ingredients in the recipes you are planning to use. Do not forget, however, to check the amounts of staples you have on hand in case there are any you do not have in sufficient quantity.

If at all possible, combine your brunch shopping list with your regular weekly list. You will save time if you can get all your shopping done in one trip. You can also save time by arranging your list according to where you expect to do your shopping—everything that you will need from the butcher shop together, from the fruit store, the bakery, etc. If you plan on doing most of your shopping at your regular supermarket, try to arrange your list according to the layout of the store so that you can follow it as you follow the aisles. This will save you a lot of steps and also make it less likely that you will forget an item or two.

Shopping for Your Brunch

Once you have established your brunch menu and made a list of the items you will need, you are ready to set out on your shopping expedition.

When you reach the store, resist the temptation to buy things that are not on your list. Do not let the appealing displays lure you into changing your thoughtfully planned menu. There is nothing to stop you, however, from making a mental note of items you may notice that are new to you or that simply did not come to mind earlier; they may serve you in good stead at a later date for another brunch.

Nor should you allow yourself to question the amounts you have decided you need. If you are like most of us, you will suffer a few last-minute pangs of doubt as to whether you have really planned on enough. Ignore them. You know that you planned carefully and that you based your quantities on proven recipes. You will not run short.

In fact, not only will there be enough of everything, you should probably expect to have more than you need. Morning appetites are not usually as hearty as evening ones, and if you absolutely must make purchases beyond those you have foreseen, the wisest course would probably be to pick up whatever you might need to make judicious use of the leftovers.

Storing Food for Your Brunch

The fact that you have to buy for a Sunday brunch does not necessarily mean that you have to resign yourself to tackling the Saturday afternoon shopping crowds in order to have everything as fresh as possible. With perhaps a few exceptions, you can make your purchases on whatever day you normally do and then make careful use of your refrigerator and freezer to retain the full flavor and nutritional value of everything you intend to serve. Of course this means following the general rules of proper storage as well as those that apply to defrosting food in the microwave oven. A little care and attention to detail at this point will save a lot of wear and tear on your nerves and produce quite exceptional results.

Refrigerating Food for Your Brunch

Care should be taken to properly wrap any item you are storing in your refrigerator, even if it is to stay there for only a short period. Plastic bags, containers covered with plastic wrap and those with lids that provide an airtight seal will not only keep the foods that are stored in them fresh, they will also prevent these items from affecting the taste of other foods in the refrigerator.

Certainly, the cool temperature of the

refrigerator will prolong the life of most foods, but this does not necessarily mean that they will emerge totally unscathed under all or any circumstances. In fact, food that is not protected from the cold air that circulates in the refrigerator will dry out and lose color, flavor and nutritional value. Moreover, as the same air is constantly recirculating, improperly packaged items will not only suffer some degree of deterioration themselves, they may well damage others. The fat on a piece of meat, for example, will oxidize quite rapidly and transmit a rancid taste to other food.

Depending on the particular item, food may be properly refrigerated in serving dishes carefully covered with plastic wrap that clings well, in tightly sealed plastic bags especially designed for this purpose, or in airtight containers.

Do not let all these cautions frighten you. It is really quite easy to refrigerate food properly, and the convenience of being able to shop and prepare ahead will more than compensate for the extra bit of time and trouble it takes.

A good many dishes that are ideal for a brunch—ham, roast beef, pâté, meat loaf, to mention just a few—can in fact be cooked a day or two ahead of time and stored in the refrigerator. Smoked meats of all sorts and smoked fish also keep very well in the refrigerator.

Desserts are another item that can be prepared ahead and kept in the refrigerator. Stewed fruit, for instance, prepared 12 hours ahead will be wonderfully tasty; breads, muffins and cakes will retain all their freshness, providing, once again, that they are carefully wrapped.

On the other hand, it is not advisable to refrigerate washed, peeled and cut up fruit or vegetables for any but the briefest length of time. Thus prepared, most such items tend to deteriorate rapidly. Fresh fruit and vegetables keep best unwashed and untrimmed. It is definitely a mistake to cut them much ahead of time and refrigerate them in water. Granted vegetables stored in this way will remain crisp, but they will lose color and much of their vitamin content.

If you remember to follow the advice outlined here, you can make efficient use of your refrigerator by buying, storing and even preparing a number of the items on your brunch menu well ahead of time, making it easier for you to relax and enjoy the company of your guests.

Freezing Food for Your Brunch

If you own a freezer, you will find it possible to plan your brunch menu in such a way that you can buy and prepare many items in advance. This of course greatly facilitates the organization of the meal —and enables you to get more enjoyment out of it.

In this respect the microwave is a definite boon, given its ability to thaw and heat food quickly, without your even having to change containers.

The principles outlined above as to proper storage take on an even greater importance in connection with freezing. The danger of food drying out and becoming discolored—a phenomenon known as freezer burn—if it is not sealed in airtight wrapping or containers is proportionately greater in the colder air of the freezer. Therefore, if food is being frozen for any length of time, one should not rely on a single layer of ordinary thin plastic wrap as it is too liable to tear when things are shifted around in the freezer.

If you are using rigid containers to store food, choose an appropriate size. If the container is too large, the excess air will allow ice crystals to form and cause the food to deteriorate. As well, round containers are preferable to square ones since they allow the contents to defrost more evenly. As for plastic bags, best of all are those that can, with proper equipment, be vacuum sealed. If you do not have such equipment, you can still get good results with plastic bags by sealing them as tightly as possible after having expelled all the air.

However you wrap your packages for the freezer, be sure to label even those you expect to use very soon with precise information as to the contents, quantity and date by which they must be used. If for some reason an item you planned for your brunch is not needed after all, you will then be able to keep track of it and make sure you use it while it is still at its best.

When planning your brunch, remember that most items to be served cooked can be blanched and frozen ahead. Most vegetable and sauce combinations can also be prepared in advance and frozen.

Uncooked meat and poultry as well as many cooked dishes —including terrines, some pâtés, fish and seafood—also freeze well and are easy to defrost. Even sausages can be frozen, but for best results we advise against freezing bacon or salami and other delicatessen meats.

Cooked pasta and rice, on the other hand, as well as pie dough (rolled or unrolled), breads, muffins, patty shells and cakes all freeze well, as do sauces and soups.

These are just a few of the ways you can combine the convenience of your freezer and your microwave oven to make the work involved in preparing a brunch easier.

Defrosting in the Microwave

Defrosting in the microwave is a precise yet quick process that allows you to retain the original appearance and the full flavor of food. Providing that the food has been frozen properly, it is easy to achieve excellent results in defrosting by following a few simple rules that we will review here.

Defrosting a Roast or a Ham

The simplest way of defrosting a roast or a ham is, of course, to set it in a dish in the refrigerator for as long as it takes to thaw it completely. There is however a major drawback to this method of defrosting: it is extremely slow and therefore requires that you know well ahead of time when you are going to want to use that particular item. It also occupies valuable space in your refrigerator, which you may not be able to spare for the amount of time required.

Defrosting in the microwave oven is much quicker and provides a perfectly acceptable alternative providing that you make sure the meat defrosts evenly. In other words, a certain amount of care must be taken to ensure that none of the meat begins to cook while part of it remains frozen. For this reason, the ends of the roast or ham must be protected because they are more exposed to the microwaves than is the center. This is very easily done by covering the ends with aluminum foil.

It is also necessary to ensure that the meat is not in contact with the juices that seep out during the defrosting process. Never forget that liquids attract microwaves and therefore quickly reach high temperatures. Any part of a roast or ham sitting in its juice would therefore begin to cook long before defrosting is complete.

To sum up, when defrosting a roast or ham, you are assured of perfect results if you abide by the following three rules:

1. Set the meat on a rack or on an upside down saucer or plate in a cooking dish. Juices will then run down to the bottom of the rack or dish and the meat itself will never be in contact with them.

2. So that the heat spreads evenly throughout the meat, divide the total time the meat is to be exposed to the microwaves into several short cycles and alternate these with standing periods, each equal to one-quarter of the total defrosting time. After each cycle, give the dish in which the meat has been placed a half-turn.

3. After the first defrosting cycle, check the meat and cover any defrosted parts—thin or bony parts will defrost more quickly than others—with aluminum foil.

Defrosting Fruits and Vegetables

There is an impressive array of frozen fruits and vegetables available in supermarkets, and these can stand you in good stead when you are preparing a brunch. It is also possible, of course, to freeze fruits and vegetables yourself. You may do this as a matter of course in the summertime, when local produce is at its best and least expensive, or you may do it specifically in view of your planned brunch in order to make the final preparations easier.

Whether you are using industrially frozen produce or that which you have packaged yourself, you will find that frozen fruits and vegetables retain their bright color and flavor when properly defrosted in the microwave. The method to be followed in defrosting is simple and can be summed up in four basic points.

1. Remove the block of fruit or vegetables from its wrapping and place it on a rack—either a bacon rack or one that sits in a baking dish. (It may be necessary to defrost briefly in the microwave before the packaging can be removed.)

2. Divide the defrosting time into several cycles and proceed with the first of these. As soon as possible, gently break up the block of fruit or vegetables with a fork. In order to make sure that none of them start to cook, transfer any that are almost thawed to the center of the dish, moving those that are still completely frozen to the edges. Remove any that are completely defrosted.

3. Allow less rather than more defrosting time in the oven than you think you need. It is always possible to add an extra defrosting cycle if necessary, whereas there is nothing much you can do to salvage fruit or vegetables that have dried out.

4. Allow a period of standing time at the end of each defrosting cycle and especially at the end of the last one. The final standing period is an integral part of the defrosting process.

Note: The defrosting method described here in connection with fruits and vegetables applies equally well to any food that is frozen in a block —seafood, cooked pasta and rice, cooked meat and poultry, etc.

Cooking in the Microwave

If you are new to microwave cooking, you may be concerned about the adjustments that you will have to make to your usual scheduling in view of the shorter cooking times required. Not to worry: a little thought and practice is all it takes.

Certainly, the use of a microwave oven considerably reduces the time required for the actual cooking of most foods. Nonetheless, cooking times will still be affected, as they are in conventional cooking, by a number of factors: the specific cut in the case of meat; the type of preparation the item has been given (in the case of vegetables, for instance, whether they have been peeled, quartered, sliced, diced, etc.); the weight or volume of the food; its temperature when placed in the oven; the intensity of heat at which it is cooked.

In the case of meat, a few factors in addition to initial temperature and cut must be taken into consideration in estimating cooking times in the microwave. In particular, the fat and moisture content, the presence of sugar (if any) and the presence and size of bone will affect the cooking time. Because fat attracts microwaves, a lean roast will cook more slowly than one covered with a layer of fat. Similarly, a ham that has been cured or glazed with sugar will cook more quickly than one that hasn't, because sugar also attracts microwaves.

Checking a Roast or Ham for Doneness

There are several ways of testing a roast or a ham cooked in the microwave for doneness. These range from measuring the internal temperature of the piece of meat, through checking for tenderness, to cutting off a slice and judging by its general appearance.

The obvious way to check the internal temperature of a roast or ham is by means of a meat thermometer, but this can also be done with a fork. Simply insert the fork into the middle of the meat, take it out and touch it with your fingers. If a lot of juice trickles out and the fork is warm, the meat is still rare. If there is little juice and the fork is hot, the meat is medium. And if there is little juice and it is clear, the meat is well done.

In checking for tenderness, if the fibers of a piece of meat can be broken apart quite easily with a fork, the meat is adequately cooked and should be tender.

The degree of doneness can also be judged quite accurately by cutting a slice off a roast. As the illustrations on the opposite page indicate, a very rare roast will have only a narrow layer of browned meat around the outside, whereas a well-done roast will be browned through the center.

Organizing Your Preparation Time

Obviously, there is a lot more involved in preparing a brunch than simply putting things in the oven to cook and then serving them. A great deal of cleaning, cutting, measuring and mixing will no doubt be required. The amount of time these steps take will vary, and it is advisable to plan the precise order in which you will do them. Some thought given to this when you are planning your brunch menu will enable you to make more efficient use of your time and your microwave oven.

If your brunch menu consists mainly of hot dishes, you would do well to plan them such that they can be served one after the other rather than all at the same time. The second dish can thus be cooking or reheating while you and your guests enjoy the first—and each other's company. Much pleasanter for all, you will agree!

Remember also that many dishes and sauces can be kept warm for quite a while without losing any of their appeal. Your conventional oven can stand you in good stead for this purpose, as can chafing dishes.

In most cases, it is probably best to plan a more-or-less equal mix of hot and cold dishes. You will find the task of preparing your brunch

VERY RARE

RARE

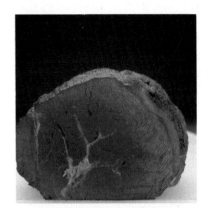

MEDIUM

WELL DONE

much lighter if you have been able to prepare a number of items—hard-boiled eggs, ham, roast beef, pâtés—a day ahead. Other items that will not keep quite so well—salads and cold hors d'oeuvres, for instance—can be prepared early in the morning of the day of the brunch and stored in the refrigerator.

To help your organize your

preparation time, each brunch in this volume is preceded by a planned guide as to when each dish should be prepared. Note, however, that we have included only the main dishes on the menu in these schedules and not those listed under "Suggestions"—dishes that may or may not be included in your meal, depending on what time and preferences permit.

A Hot Brunch

Autumn: the leaves turn gold and red, the air is crisp with a touch of frost and the hint of snow and bitter winds to come. A very beautiful time of year, but one that most of us greet with mixed feelings. Winter will bring its own pleasures, but at this time they seem far less real than those of the summer that is ending.

What better way to dispel the inevitable feelings of melancholy that autumn brings than by gathering a few good friends to share the warming effects of a hearty meal and comfortable conversation around a cozy fire?

The brunch menu we propose here will help you achieve the relaxed sense of well-being that you want to create. It begins very simply with coleslaw and a delicious cream of asparagus soup. This is followed first by an unforgettable vegetable and shrimp platter, then by ham cooked in beer and a delightful concoction of eggs, artichoke hearts and crabmeat with béarnaise sauce.

For dessert we suggest a seasonable dish of lightly cooked apples with Gruyère cheese and, if you are feeling lavish, a magnificent Queen Elizabeth cake with a coconut-flavored sauce. Finally, Irish coffee will provide the perfect, convivial ending to your autumn brunch.

The day before the brunch:
—Cook the ham, the vegetables and the shrimps.
The morning of the brunch:
—Prepare the apples but do not cook them (coat with lemon juice); arrange the vegetable and shrimp platter.
40 minutes before the brunch:
—Make the béarnaise sauce and prepare the egg surprise.
10 minutes before the brunch:
—Cook the apples.

Coleslaw

Ingredients
1 green cabbage, finely chopped
3 carrots, grated
150 mL (2/3 cup) mayonnaise
50 mL (1/4 cup) vinegar
75 mL (1/3 cup) honey
pepper to taste

Method
— Place the cabbage and carrots in a bowl and mix; set aside.
— To prepare the dressing, combine the mayonnaise and the vinegar; add the honey and the pepper and mix well.
— Pour the dressing over the vegetables and mix well.
— Refrigerate for 2 hours before serving.

Cream of Asparagus Soup

Ingredients
450 g (1 lb) fresh asparagus
60 mL (4 tablespoons) butter
1 onion, finely chopped
75 mL (1/3 cup) flour
1 L (4 cups) chicken stock
15 mL (1 tablespoon) chives, chopped
125 mL (1/2 cup) 18% cream
15 mL (1 tablespoon) lemon juice
2 mL (1/2 teaspoon) paprika
salt and pepper to taste

Method
— Cut the asparagus into pieces, setting aside a few tips to use as garnish.
— Put the butter in a dish and heat at 100% for 1 minute to melt.
— Add the onion and the asparagus.
— Cover and cook at 100% for 4 to 5 minutes.
— Add the flour and stir.
— Stir in the chicken stock.
— Cover and cook at 100% for 10 minutes, stirring 3 times during the cooking time.
— Pour into the blender and blend for a few seconds until smooth.
— Add the chives, cream, lemon juice and paprika; stir with a spoon.
— Season to taste and heat for 3 to 4 minutes at 100%, stirring halfway through the cooking time; set aside.
— Place the reserved asparagus tips in a dish with a little water and heat at 100% for 2 minutes to blanch.
— Garnish the soup with the asparagus tips before serving.

Vegetable and Shrimp Platter

Ingredients
1 small cauliflower, whole
225 g (8 oz) snow peas
450 g (1 lb) asparagus
225 g (8 oz) medium shrimps,
shelled
175 mL (3/4 cup) mayonnaise
225 g (8 oz) cherry tomatoes
1 284 mL (10 oz) can hearts of
palm

Vinaigrette:*
125 mL (1/2 cup) vinegar
7 mL (1-1/2 teaspoons) salt
10 mL (2 teaspoons) Dijon
mustard
2 cloves garlic, finely chopped
375 mL (1-1/2 cups) oil

* The vinaigrette will be even
tastier if it is prepared a few
hours in advance.

Method
— Place the whole
cauliflower in a dish and
add 50 mL (1/4 cup) of
water; cover and cook at
100% for 8 to 12 minutes
or until done to your
liking, giving the dish a
half-turn midway through
the cooking time. Drain
the cauliflower and leave
to cool.
— Put the snow peas in a dish
and add 50 mL (1/4 cup)
of water; cover and cook
at 100% for 3 to 5
minutes. Drain and set
aside to cool.
— Put the asparagus in a dish
and add 50 mL (1/4 cup)
of water; cover and cook
at 100% for 4 to 6
minutes, giving the dish a
half-turn midway through
the cooking time. Drain

and set aside to cool.
— Place the shrimps in a
dish, cover and cook at
70% for 4 to 5 minutes,
giving the dish a half-turn
midway through the
cooking time. Leave to
cool.
— Set the cauliflower in the
center of a serving platter
and spoon the
mayonnaise over it.
— Arrange the shrimps and
the other vegetables
attractively around the
cauliflower.
— To prepare the vinaigrette,
combine the vinegar, salt,
mustard and garlic; add
the oil while beating
constantly with a wire
whisk.
— Spoon the vinaigrette over
the vegetables before
serving.

Ham in Beer

Level of Difficulty	🍴
Preparation Time	5 min*
Cost per Serving	$
Number of Servings	10
Nutritional Value	506 calories 45.1 g protein 20.8 g carbohydrate
Food Exchanges	7 oz meat
Cooking Time	1 h 30 min
Standing Time	None
Power Level	50%
Write Your Cooking Time Here	🍎✏️

* The ham should be cooled before serving.

Ingredients
1 ham, 2.7 kg (6 lb)
1 284 mL (10 oz) bottle beer
10 mL (2 teaspoons) mustard powder

Method
— Put the ham in a cooking bag and place in a dish.
— Mix the mustard powder and beer and pour into the bag.
— Close the bag, leaving a small opening through which steam can escape.
— Cook for 45 minutes at 50%.
— Turn the ham over.
— Continue to cook at 50% for a further 30 to 45 minutes, or until the ham is cooked.
— Allow the ham to cool before serving.

Always a winner, ham is very quickly prepared with a minimum number of ingredients.

Mix the beer and mustard powder and pour into the cooking bag.

Close the bag loosely, leaving a small opening through which steam can escape.

MICROTIPS

Instead of Twist Ties

If you have no plastic twist ties, simply cut a narrow strip off the cooking bag. Tie this around the open end of the bag, but not too tightly. Enough of an opening should be left to allow steam to escape.

Egg Surprise

Level of Difficulty	🍴🍴
Preparation Time	30 min
Cost per Serving	$ $
Number of Servings	10
Nutritional Value	322 calories 12.9 g protein 2.2 mg iron
Food Exchanges	2 oz meat 1 vegetable exchange 3-1/2 fat exchanges
Cooking Time	25 min
Standing Time	None
Power Level	100%, 70%
Write Your Cooking Time Here	

Ingredients
2.5 L (10 cups) water
125 mL (1/2 cup) vinegar
10 eggs
10 artichoke hearts
225 g (8 oz) crabmeat
375 mL (1-1/2 cups) béarnaise sauce

Method
— Add half the vinegar to half the water and heat at 100% for 6 to 7 minutes or until it boils.
— Beginning with 5 eggs, carefully break one at a time into a small bowl and tip it gently into the boiling water.
— Pierce the yolk and white of each egg in two or three places with a toothpick and cook at 100% for 4 minutes.
— Carefully remove each egg with a slotted spoon and plunge into cold water; discard the boiling water.
— Repeat the operation with the remaining 5 eggs and the rest of the water and vinegar.
— Arrange the artichoke hearts on a serving platter, spoon equal amounts of crabmeat over each one and top with a poached egg.
— Heat at 70% for 2 to 3 minutes.
— Heat the béarnaise sauce, pour over the eggs and serve.

MICROTIPS

Storing Eggs

Eggs do not have to be kept at very low temperatures. They will keep quite well in the least cold sections of the refrigerator—provided, however, that the temperature remains constant. They can safely be left in the containers in which eggs are normally bought, or you may prefer to transfer them if your refrigerator is equipped with egg racks. In the latter case, you must make sure to place them as they are placed in their cartons, that is, with the more pointed end down, so that the air pocket at the rounded end is maintained and the yolk remains well centered in the egg. Thus placed, eggs will keep for up to two months in the refrigerator.

You should also be aware that eggshells are porous and do not provide complete protection against odors. It is therefore advisable to avoid placing any food with strong odors near the eggs. Of course, because of the circulation of air in the refrigerator, such foods should always be stored in covered containers or airtight wrapping.

Queen Elizabeth Cake

Ingredients
250 mL (1 cup) dates
250 mL (1 cup) hot water
50 mL (1/4 cup) butter
250 mL (1 cup) sugar
2 eggs, beaten
5 mL (1 teaspoon) vanilla
375 mL (1-1/2 cups) flour
5 mL (1 teaspoon) baking soda
5 mL (1 teaspoon) baking powder

Sauce:
250 mL (1 cup) brown sugar
250 mL (1 cup) coconut, grated
60 mL (4 tablespoons) 35% cream
150 mL (2/3 cup) butter

Method
— To make the cake, combine the dates and the hot water in a dish and heat at 100% for 3 minutes, or until the mixture boils; set aside to cool, and put through the blender to purée (optional).
— Combine the butter, sugar, beaten eggs and vanilla in a bowl; mix until creamy.
— Add the flour, baking soda and baking powder and mix well.
— Add the dates, mix thoroughly and pour the batter into a ring dish.
— Place the dish on a rack in the oven and cook at 70% for 10 to 12 minutes, giving the dish a half-turn midway through the cooking time.
— Meanwhile, combine all the sauce ingredients in a dish and stir.
— Heat at 100% for 3 minutes, until it boils.
— Pour the sauce over the cake and heat for 40 to 60 seconds before serving.

Irish Coffee

Ingredients
45 mL (3 tablespoons) Irish whiskey
10 mL (2 teaspoons) sugar
strong coffee
whipped cream

Method
— Frost the edges of the cup with sugar.
— Pour the whisky into the cup and add coffee until 2/3 full.
— Garnish with a generous dollop of whipped cream and serve as is, without stirring.

Apples with Gruyère Cheese

Ingredients
5 large apples
250 mL (1 cup) Gruyère
cheese, grated
paprika to garnish

Method
— Peel and core the apples.
— Cut the apples in half.
— Arrange the halves on a microwave-safe platter; sprinkle with the grated cheese and then some paprika.
— Cook at 90% for 3 to 4 minutes, giving the platter a half-turn midway through the cooking time.
— Allow to stand for 2 minutes before serving.

Level of Difficulty	🍴
Preparation Time	15 min
Cost per Serving	$
Number of Servings	10
Nutritional Value	77 calories 9.2 g carbohydrate 7.9 mg calcium
Food Exchanges	1/2 fruit exchange 1/2 milk exchange
Cooking Time	4 min
Standing Time	2 min
Power Level	90%
Write Your Cooking Time Here	

A Birthday Brunch

An evening dinner or other party is the most common way to celebrate a birthday. It may or may not come as a surprise to the guest of honor, and it will probably be successful: everyone will have a good time. Nonetheless, there is something very predictable about such a party and you may find yourself wishing you could think of some more original way to celebrate an important birthday.

If so, you will certainly welcome our suggestions for an extra special birthday brunch. The novelty of the idea and the relaxed atmosphere combined with the delectable array of dishes we have planned for your menu will delight your guests and make the occasion a truly unforgettable one.

Our menu for a birthday brunch begins with a cold macaroni salad and asparagus on toast. These are followed first by headcheese and a wonderfully light watercress soup, then by a main course designed to satisfy the heartiest appetites: chicken

breasts supreme and egg and salmon loaf. For dessert a cake is, of course, absolutely essential, and we suggest a sumptuous layered strawberry-lime confection that is as impressive as it is delicious. As an alternative for lighter appetites, you might also wish to provide a yoghurt and blueberry cup. For a final, slightly daring touch, close your brunch with a generous serving of golden punch.

The day before the brunch:
—Prepare and cook the cake, headcheese and the chicken breasts.
The morning of the brunch:
—Prepare the yoghurt sauce; prepare the egg and salmon loaf but do not cook immediately.
40 minutes before the brunch:
—Reheat the chicken at 70% for 20 minutes, stirring twice during the cooking time; cover and leave to stand until it is time to serve it.
12 minutes before the brunch:
—Cook the egg and salmon loaf; place the blueberries in the parfait glasses but do not add the sauce until just before serving.

SUGGESTIONS

Macaroni Salad

Ingredients
1 L (4 cups) short cut
macaroni, cooked
1/2 head of lettuce, thinly
sliced
125 mL (1/2 cup) stuffed
olives, drained and chopped
250 mL (1 cup) celery, diced
50 mL (1/4 cup) radishes,
finely chopped
2 cloves garlic, crushed
125 mL (1/2 cup) orange
cheddar cheese, grated
salt and pepper to taste
mayonnaise to taste

Method
— Place the macaroni and all
the vegetables in a salad
bowl; mix well.
— Gradually add the cheese
while stirring; season to
taste.
— Add the mayonnaise and
stir until thoroughly
mixed.
— Refrigerate for 6 hours
before serving.

Asparagus on Toast

Ingredients
4 spears of white asparagus,
cooked
1 egg yolk
15 mL (1 tablespoon) boiling
water
30 mL (2 tablespoons) 35%
cream
15 mL (1 tablespoon) lemon
juice
salt and pepper to taste
1 round toasted bread
1 slice prosciutto ham, cut
into thin strips

Method
— In a small bowl, combine
the egg yolk and boiling
water; beat with a fork
until thoroughly mixed.
— Whip the cream and add to
the egg yolk; add the
lemon juice, salt and
pepper.
— Arrange the asparagus
spears on the toasted
bread and cover with the
sauce.
— Garnish with the
prosciutto before serving.

Watercress Soup

Ingredients
6 large sprigs of watercress,
washed and chopped
30 mL (2 tablespoons) butter
1/2 onion, finely chopped
5 potatoes, peeled and thinly
sliced
1 mL (1/4 teaspoon) tarragon
1.25 L (5 cups) chicken broth
pinch thyme
pinch rosemary
salt and pepper to taste

Method
— Put the butter and onion in
a dish and cook at 100%
for 1 minute.
— Add the potatoes,
tarragon, 125 mL (1/2
cup) of the chicken broth
and seasoning.
— Cover and cook at 100%
for 6 minutes, stirring
halfway through the
cooking time.
— Add the rest of the chicken
broth and the watercress.
— Cover and cook at 100%
for 10 minutes, stirring
halfway through the
cooking time.
— Allow to stand for 4
minutes.

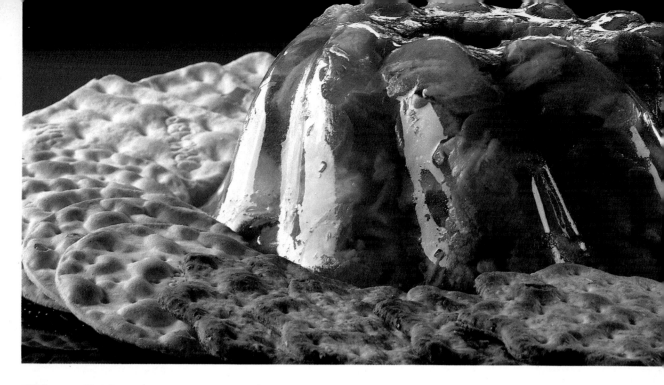

Headcheese

Ingredients

6 pigs' trotters, split in two
6 cloves
15 mL (1 tablespoon) cinnamon

15 mL (1 tablespoon) salt
2 onions, chopped
1 carrot, grated
2 L (8 cups) water

Method

— Wrap the pigs' trotters and cloves in cheesecloth and place in a deep dish.
— Add the other ingredients and cover.
— Cook at 100% for 1 to 1-1/2 hours.
— Remove the pigs' trotters and bone them; chop the meat coarsely.
— Replace the meat in the hot cooking liquid.
— Heat at 100% for 10 to 15 minutes, until it boils.
— Pour into a mold or into ramekins.
— Refrigerate for 3 hours before serving.

Level of Difficulty	🍴🍴
Preparation Time	1 h*
Cost per Serving	$
Number of Servings	18
Nutritional Value	70.3 calories 7.6 g protein
Food Exchanges	1 oz meat
Cooking Time	1 h 45 min
Standing Time	None
Power Level	100%
Write Your Cooking Time Here	

* The headcheese must be refrigerated for 3 hours before serving.

Chicken Breasts Supreme

Level of Difficulty	
Preparation Time	20 min
Cost per Serving	$
Number of Servings	10
Nutritional Value	164 calories 13.2 g protein 8 mg iron
Food Exchanges	1.5 oz meat 1/2 vegetable exchange 1-1/2 fat exchanges
Cooking Time	19 min
Standing Time	3 min
Power Level	100%, 70%
Write Your Cooking Time Here	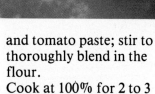

Ingredients
3 whole chicken breasts, boned and skinned
90 mL (6 tablespoons) butter
284 g (10 oz) mushrooms, halved
90 mL (6 tablespoons) flour
1 L (4 cups) chicken broth, heated
50 mL (1/4 cup) tomato paste
90 mL (6 tablespoons) cheddar cheese, grated
lemon juice
salt and pepper to taste

Method
— Cube the chicken breasts.
— Preheat a browning dish at 100% for 7 minutes; add half the butter and heat at 100% for 30 seconds.
— Sear the chicken cubes.
— Lower the power level to 70% and cook for 4 to 6 minutes; remove the chicken and set aside.
— Put the rest of the butter and the mushrooms in the browning dish.
— Cook at 100% for 3 to 4 minutes, stirring once.
— Add the flour and mix well.
— Stir in the chicken broth and tomato paste; stir to thoroughly blend in the flour.
— Cook at 100% for 2 to 3 minutes, stirring once during the cooking time.
— Blend the cheddar cheese into the sauce.
— Add the chicken, lemon juice and seasoning.
— Cover and cook at 70% for 4 to 6 minutes, stirring midway through the cooking time.
— Allow to stand for 3 minutes.

Begin by assembling the required ingredients.

Add the flour to the butter and mushrooms and mix well.

Add the chicken, lemon juice and seasoning to the sauce and continue to cook according to instructions.

Egg and Salmon Loaf

Level of Difficulty	
Preparation Time	20 min
Cost per Serving	$
Number of Servings	10
Nutritional Value	197 calories 14.2 g protein 4.5 mg iron
Food Exchanges	2 oz meat 1/2 bread exchange 1/4 fat exchange
Cooking Time	12 min
Standing Time	2 min
Power Level	70%
Write Your Cooking Time Here	

Ingredients
1 398 mL (14 oz) can salmon, drained
6 eggs, lightly beaten
500 mL (2 cups) breadcrumbs
125 mL (1/2 cup) 18% cream
250 mL (1 cup) celery, diced
50 mL (1/4 cup) onion, grated
30 mL (2 tablespoons) lemon juice
30 mL (2 tablespoons) parsley

Method
— Combine all the ingredients except the parsley in a bowl and mix until well blended.
— Spoon the mixture into 10 ramekins.
— Sprinkle with the parsley.
— Arrange 5 ramekins on a raised rack and cook at 70% for 5 to 6 minutes, giving each ramekin a half-turn midway through the cooking time. Repeat with the 5 remaining ramekins.
— Allow to stand for 2 minutes.

These are the ingredients you will need to prepare this sure-to-please recipe.

MICROTIPS

How to Test Eggs for Freshness

It is not necessary to break an egg to tell whether it is fresh. One way you can test an unbroken egg for freshness is to shake it gently near your ear. If you can detect movement of the contents within the shell, it means that it has been quite a while since the egg was laid. This is explained by the fact that the eggshell is porous and moisture from within is gradually lost. Therefore, with time, the air pocket inside the shell gets larger and the displacement of the egg itself becomes noticeable.

You can also test for freshness by putting the egg in water. The older the egg, the larger the air space inside the shell and the closer it will come to floating. Thus, a fresh egg will settle horizontally at the bottom of the container of water, whereas a less fresh egg will tend to drift towards a more vertical position. An egg that is two or three weeks old will stand on end when placed in water.

As you can see, eggs dry out fairly quickly and it is therefore important to buy the freshest possible.

SUGGESTIONS

Strawberry-Lime Chiffon Cake

Ingredients
1 envelope strawberry-
flavored jello powder
dissolved in 250 mL (1 cup)
boiling water
1 envelope lime-flavored jello
powder dissolved in
250 mL (1 cup) boiling water
5 large eggs
250 mL (1 cup) sugar
50 mL (1/4 cup) oil
250 mL (1 cup) flour
10 mL (2 teaspoons) baking
powder
pinch salt
5 mL (1 teaspoon) lemon
extract
500 mL (2 cups) 35% cream
50 mL (1/4 cup) fruit sugar

Method
— Separate the eggs.
— Beat the egg whites until
  stiff; add the sugar and
  then beat the yolks and
  fold into the whites.
— Add the oil.
— Sift the flour with the
  baking powder and salt
  and add to the egg
  mixture along with the
  lemon extract.
— Line two round molds
  with waxed paper and
  pour equal amounts of
  batter into each.
— Cook the cakes one at a
  time: set on a raised rack
  in the oven and cook at
  70% for 3 minutes.
— Give the cake a half-turn
  and cook for another 2 to

4 minutes at 70%.
— Leave the cakes to cool
  completely.
— Dissolve the packets of
  jello powder as instructed
  and pour the strawberry
  over one cake and the lime
  over the other.
— Allow the liquid jello to
  soak into the cakes and
  then refrigerate for 6
  hours until set.
— Prepare the topping for
  the cake just prior to
  serving.
— Whip the cream while
  gradually adding the fruit
  sugar.
— Spread the whipped cream
  over the cakes and place
  one on top of the other.

Golden Punch*

Ingredients
2 bottles champagne
1 bottle sweet white wine
(sauterne type)
1 bottle soda water
2 trays ice cubes
60 mL (2 oz) cognac
60 mL (2 oz) cointreau
50 mL (1/4 cup) maple syrup
250 mL (1 cup) strawberries,
thinly sliced
fresh mint leaves

Method
— In a large bowl, mix the
  champagne, white wine
  and soda water;
  refrigerate for 12 hours.
— Place the ice cubes in a
  punch bowl.
— Pour the cognac, cointreau
  and maple syrup over the

ice cubes and stir.
— Add the champagne
  mixture and stir well.
— Garnish with strawberries
  and mint leaves before
  serving.

* Yields 36 125 mL (4 oz) servings.

Blueberries with Yoghurt and Honey

Ingredients

1.25 L (5 cups) fresh blueberries

375 mL (1-1/2 cups) plain yoghurt

50 mL (1/4 cup) liquid honey

5 mL (1 teaspoon) lemon zest

5 mL (1 teaspoon) cinnamon

2 mL (1/2 teaspoon) nutmeg

Level of Difficulty	🍴
Preparation Time	10 min
Cost per Serving	$ $
Number of Servings	10
Nutritional Value	93 calories 19.6 g carbohydrate 74.7 mg calcium
Food Exchanges	1 fruit exchange 1/4 milk exchange
Cooking Time	None
Standing Time	None
Power Level	None
Write Your Cooking Time Here	

Method

— Prepare the sauce by combining all the ingredients except the blueberries.

— Distribute the blueberries among 10 parfait glasses. Pour the sauce over them and serve.

An Easter Brunch

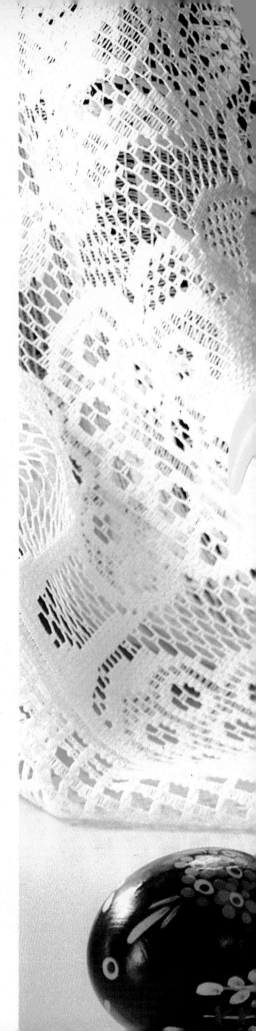

Next to Christmas, Easter is certainly our most festive and widely celebrated holiday. Equally certainly, some of the joy with which we celebrate it is due to its timing. Even when it arrives early, most of us see Easter as the end—or at least the beginning of the end —of our long winter. It brings with it the promise of sunshine and budding trees —cause indeed to celebrate!

There is also a much more mundane reason why Easter Sunday is the ideal occasion for a festive brunch; coming as it does in the midst of a three- or four-day weekend, preparation can be done at a more leisurely pace and you can therefore relax and take as much pleasure in the occasion as you provide for your guests.

In the following pages you will find some of the most appropriate and delicious dishes that could possibly be served for an Easter brunch. We suggest beginning with a cheese platter complemented by a refreshing cucumber salad. Next come poached eggs served on an asparagus mousse, followed by an extraordinary ham and egg terrine and exquisite seafood vol-au-vents. For dessert, strawberry trifle and rhubarb tart give a delightful foretaste of summer delights to come, especially when they are accompanied by a pineapple salad served with sparkling wine or orange juice.

The day before the brunch:
—Prepare the ham and egg terrine and the strawberry trifle.
The morning of the brunch:
—Arrange and refrigerate the cheese platter.
40 minutes before the brunch:
—Take the cheese platter out of the refrigerator.
30 minutes before the brunch:
—Prepare the seafood filling for the vol-au-vents.

SUGGESTIONS

Cucumber Salad

Ingredients
3 large cucumbers
250 mL (1 cup) boiling water
15 mL (1 tablespoon) sugar
10 mL (2 teaspoons) salt
freshly ground pepper (12 twists of the pepper mill)
30 mL (2 tablespoons) vinegar

Method
— Peel the cucumbers and cut them in two lengthwise.
— Scoop the seeds out of the cucumber halves with a spoon; slice the halves very thinly and set aside.
— In a bowl, combine the water, sugar, salt, pepper and vinegar.
— Add the sliced cucumbers and cover. (Cover should be airtight.)
— Refrigerate for 12 hours.
— Drain the cucumbers and serve on a bed of lettuce leaves.

Poached Eggs on Asparagus Mousse

Ingredients
10 eggs
900 g (2 lb) asparagus
50 mL (1/4 cup) water (for cooking the asparagus)
2.5 L (10 cups) boiling water (for cooking the eggs)
125 mL (1/2 cup) vinegar

Hollandaise Sauce:
See the recipe on page 12 of *Sauces and Soups,* Volume 11

Method
— Prepare the hollandaise sauce and set aside.
— Wash the asparagus and cut into 2.5 cm (1 in) lengths.
— Place the asparagus in a dish, add the water and cook at 100% for 10 to 12 minutes, stirring once.
— Drain the asparagus and put in the blender; blend for a few seconds to purée and gradually add 125 mL (1/2 cup) hollandaise sauce.
— Add a little more hollandaise so that the mousse becomes pale green in color without being too liquid; set the mousse and the rest of the hollandaise aside.
— Beginning with 5 eggs, carefully break one egg at a time into a small bowl and tip gently into a dish containing half the boiling water and half the vinegar; pierce the yolks and whites in a few places with a toothpick and cook at 100% for 4 to 5 minutes.
— Remove the eggs with a slotted spoon and plunge into cold water.
— Repeat the process with the remaining 5 eggs.
— Trim the eggs decoratively and set aside.
— Place an equal amount of the mousse on each of 10 small plates; make a small hollow in the center of the mousse and place a poached egg in it.
— Heat at 70% for 2 to 3 minutes and spoon a little hollandaise sauce over each egg before serving.

Cheese Tray

Ingredients
225 g (8 oz) brie
225 g (8 oz) Gruyère
225 g (8 oz) blue cheese
225 g (8 oz) cheddar
225 g (8 oz) Gouda
225 g (8 oz) oka
fruit of your choice

Method
— Cut the cheeses according to your preference. Possibilities include wedges, cubes, strips.
— Arrange on a serving platter and garnish with fruit.
— You may want to warm briefly at 30% to bring the cheeses to room temperature.

Level of Difficulty	🍴
Preparation Time	10 min
Cost per Serving	$ $
Number of Servings	10
Nutritional Value	493 calories 31.2 g protein 780 mg calcium
Food Exchanges	4.5 oz meat 1-1/4 milk exchanges
Cooking Time	Optional
Standing Time	None
Power Level	30%
Write Your Cooking Time Here	

Ham and Egg Terrine

Level of Difficulty	🍴🍴🍴
Preparation Time	30 min
Cost per Serving	$
Number of Servings	10
Nutritional Value	409 calories 21.7 g protein 3.2 mg iron
Food Exchanges	2.5 oz meat 1/2 vegetable exchange 1 bread exchange 2-1/2 fat exchanges
Cooking Time	42 min
Standing Time	None
Power Level	100%, 50%
Write Your Cooking Time Here	🍎✏️

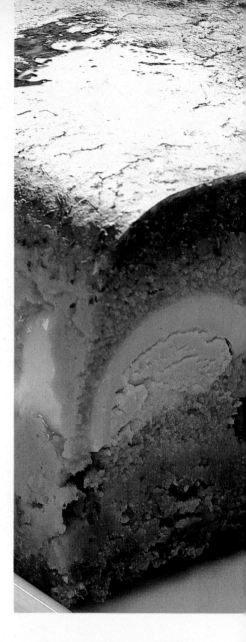

Ingredients
450 g (1 lb) ham, ground
225 g (8 oz) asparagus
30 mL (2 tablespoons) water
4 egg whites
400 mL (1-2/3 cups) 35%
cream
50 mL (1/4 cup) sherry
1.125 L (4-1/2 cups) Italian
breadcrumbs
175 mL (3/4 cup) chicken
broth
1 onion, grated
284 g (10 oz) cooked spinach,
drained
salt and pepper to taste
10 mL (2 teaspoons) Dijon
mustard
5 eggs, hard-boiled

Method
— Place the asparagus in a
dish, add the water, cover
and cook at 100% for 4 to
6 minutes.
— Drain the asparagus and
allow to cool.
— Combine the ham and 1
egg white in a blender and
gradually add 150 mL
(2/3 cup) of the cream.
— Blend for a few seconds
until the mixture is
smooth.
— Drizzle in the sherry and
mix; cover and
refrigerate.
— Combine the breadcrumbs
and broth in a 2 L (8 cup)
bowl; cook at 100% for 8

to 10 minutes, or until the
mixture thickens, stirring
twice during the cooking
time.
— Let cool.
— Put the onion in a dish,
cover and cook for 1
minute at 100%.
— Put two-thirds of the
breadcrumb and broth
mixture in the blender and
add two egg whites, the
onion, the spinach and the
seasoning.
— Turn on the blender and
gradually add 125 mL

(1/2 cup) of 35% cream; blend until smooth.
— Cover and refrigerate.
— Put the rest of the breadcrumb mixture into the blender with one egg white and the mustard; blend briefly, add the rest of the cream and beat until smooth.
— Grease a 25 x 12 cm (10 x 5 in) loaf dish.
— Spread half the breadcrumb and spinach mixture in the bottom of the dish and cover with

half the ham mixture.
— Cut the hard-boiled eggs in half, place cut side up on the ham; cover with the rest of the ham mixture and smooth out with a spatula.
— Arrange the asparagus on the ham and cover with the breadcrumb and mustard mixture.
— Smooth out and cover with the remaining breadcrumb and spinach mixture.
— Smooth out again and

cover with plastic wrap, leaving a small opening on the side so that steam can escape.
— Place the dish on a raised rack in the oven and cook at 50% for 20 to 25 minutes, giving the dish a half-turn midway through the cooking time.
— Allow to cool and refrigerate before serving.

Seafood Vol-au-Vents

Level of Difficulty	
Preparation Time	15 min
Cost per Serving	$ $
Number of Servings	10
Nutritional Value	632 calories 27.7 g protein 385 mg calcium
Food Exchanges	3.5 oz meat 1/2 milk exchange 2-1/2 bread exchanges 3-1/2 fat exchanges
Cooking Time	20 min
Standing Time	None
Power Level	100%, 70%
Write Your Cooking Time Here	

Ingredients
450 g (1 lb) scallops
450 g (1 lb) shrimps, shelled
175 mL (3/4 cup) butter
175 mL (3/4 cup) flour
750 mL (3 cups) milk
340 g (12 oz) Gruyère cheese, grated
1 mL (1/4 teaspoon) garlic powder
salt and pepper to taste
1 mL (1/4 teaspoon) mustard powder
5 mL (1 teaspoon) tomato paste
15 mL (3 teaspoons) lemon juice
10 patty shells

Method
— Melt the butter at 100% for 1 to 1-1/2 minutes.
— Add the flour and mix; add the milk and mix well.
— Cook at 100% for 6 to 8 minutes, stirring every 2 minutes.
— Add the cheese, garlic powder, salt, pepper, mustard powder, tomato paste and 10 mL (2 teaspoons) of lemon juice; set aside.
— Arrange the shrimps and scallops in a dish and sprinkle with 5 mL (1 teaspoon) of lemon juice; cover and cook at 100% for 5 to 7 minutes.
— Remove the cooked shrimps and scallops and add them to the sauce. If the sauce is too thick, add the liquid from the cooked seafood and, if necessary, a little milk.
— Heat the sauce at 70% for 2 to 3 minutes, stirring once.
— Pour the mixture into the patty shells and serve.

MICROTIPS

The Versatile Patty Shell

Patty shells—hollowed out rounds of puff pastry—can be made from scratch but are readily available from most bakeries or frozen in packages from your supermarket. If you are using frozen patty shells, cook according to the instructions on the package. Ready-to-serve patty shells are usually best heated up briefly just before serving.

A wide variety of ingredients may serve as the basis for a vol-au-vent filling. Seafood (shrimps, scallops, lobster, crab, etc.) in a white or cheese sauce is probably the most popular, but there are many other possibilities. A salmon or sole vol-au-vent is sure to please, or you may use veal, veal sweetbreads, ham, game, poultry or mushrooms, or a combination of two or three of these or other ingredients. Surprising as it may seem, even spaghetti with tomato sauce can be used as a vol-au-vent filling.

About the only rule to remember when preparing vol-au-vents is to wait until the last minute to fill the patty shells. If you fill them too soon, the sauce will make the pastry soggy, whereas it should remain crisp and flaky.

SUGGESTIONS

Pineapple Salad

Ingredients
1 large ripe pineapple
500 mL (2 cups) fresh fruit of your choice
75 mL (1/3 cup) kirsch
75 mL (1/3 cup) icing sugar

Method
— Cut the pineapple in two lengthwise.
— Hollow out the pineapple, reserving the juice.
— Cut up the pineapple and other fresh fruit appropriately and mix.
— Spoon equal amounts of fruit into the pineapple halves.
— Sprinkle on the pineapple juice and kirsch; dust with the icing sugar before serving.

Rhubarb Tart

Ingredients
Crust:
125 mL (1/2 cup) butter
75 mL (1/3 cup) sugar
2 egg yolks
500 mL (2 cups) whole wheat flour
5 mL (1 teaspoon) baking powder
2 mL (1/2 teaspoon) salt

Filling:
1.5 L (6 cups) rhubarb, fresh or frozen, cut in 2.5 cm (1 in) pieces
50 mL (1/4 cup) water
125 mL (1/2 cup) sugar
2 mL (1/2 teaspoon) cinnamon
30 mL (2 tablespoons) cornstarch
6 eggs
500 mL (2 cups) sour cream
125 mL (1/2 cup) brown sugar, packed
10 mL (2 teaspoons) zest of lemon
2 mL (1/2 teaspoon) vanilla

Method
— To prepare the crust, beat the butter in a bowl and gradually add the sugar; cream the mixture until light and fluffy.
— Add the egg yolks and beat until the mixture is frothy; set aside.
— Sift the flour, baking powder and salt; add to the butter and egg mixture and blend thoroughly.
— Grease a circular mold and line with waxed paper; pour the batter into the mold and spread evenly.
— Place on a raised rack in the oven and cook at 70% for 4 to 6 minutes; set aside.
— To prepare the filling, put the rhubarb and the water in a dish; stir in the sugar, cinnamon and cornstarch and mix well.
— Cover and cook at 100% for 7 to 9 minutes, stirring several times during cooking.
— Allow to cool and pour into the crust; set aside.
— In a bowl, beat the eggs until pale yellow in color.
— Add the sour cream, brown sugar, lemon zest and vanilla; mix well and pour over the rhubarb.
— Place on a raised rack in the oven.
— Cook at 70% for 10 to 12 minutes, giving the dish a half-turn midway through the cooking time.
— Allow to cool, cover and refrigerate for 3 hours.

Strawberry Trifle

Ingredients
750 mL (3 cups) fresh
strawberries
125 mL (1/2 cup) sugar
50 mL (1/4 cup) cornstarch
30 mL (2 tablespoons) flour
1 L (4 cups) milk
8 egg yolks
50 mL (1/4 cup) butter
5 mL (1 teaspoon) vanilla
10 slices strawberry jelly roll

Method
— Combine the sugar,
cornstarch and flour in a
bowl; mix in the milk.
— Cook at 100% for 8 to 10
minutes, or until
thickened, stirring every 2
minutes.
— Beat the egg yolks, add
125 mL (1/2 cup) of the
hot mixture and stir
vigorously.
— Add to the rest of the hot
mixture and stir.
— Blend in the butter and

vanilla.
— Place plastic wrap directly
on the surface of the
pudding and leave to cool.
— Arrange the slices of jelly
roll in the bottom of a
large bowl and add two-
thirds of the strawberries.
— Cover with the cooled
pudding and garnish with
the remaining
strawberries.
— Refrigerate for 1 hour
before serving.

A Canadian Brunch

You have visitors from abroad and you would like to treat them to some typically Canadian dishes, but try as you may, you cannot think of anything much that seems both appropriate and uniquely Canadian. Stop worrying and remember that one of the chief qualities of Canadian ''cuisine'' is its eclectic nature and another is the general year-round availability of a wide variety of fresh and frozen produce.

The brunch menu we propose takes full advantage of both these characteristics while adding, here and there, a truly distinctive Canadian touch. We are sure it will delight your most finicky guests.

Our Canadian brunch opens with an herb-flavored green salad and grapefruit halves with rum. Next we serve beets julienne and a broccoli and cheese casserole. Ham baked in maple syrup and chicken and leek pies make an irresistible main course, while a daring orange charlotte for dessert provides a touch of the unexpected. A maple pie may be added as an alternative for those who are eager for a dessert with a distinctively Canadian flavor. Hot cider and coffee are all that is needed to make this magnificent brunch complete.

The day before the brunch:
—Cook the ham; prepare the orange charlotte; cook the chicken and vegetables and prepare the sauce for the chicken and leek pies.
The morning of the brunch:
—Prepare the grapefruit with rum but do not cook immediately.
30 minutes before the brunch:
—Reheat the sauce for the chicken pies at 100% for 4 to 5 minutes, stirring twice during the cooking time; reheat the vegetables at 70% for 3 to 4 minutes; put the chicken, vegetables and sauce into the pie crusts.
15 minutes before the brunch:
—Cook the chicken pies at 70% for 5 minutes.
5 minutes before the brunch:
—Cook the grapefruit.

SUGGESTIONS

Green Salad with Herbs

Ingredients
2 bunches cress
2 heads Boston lettuce
250 mL (1 cup) parsley,
coarsely chopped
50 mL (1/4 cup) chives,
chopped

Vinaigrette:
50 mL (1/4 cup) white wine
vinegar
50 mL (1/4 cup) lemon juice
10 mL (2 teaspoons) honey
5 mL (1 teaspoon) Dijon
mustard
250 mL (1 cup) oil
salt and pepper to taste

Method
— Wash, dry and tear up the
  cress and lettuce and place
  in a salad bowl.
— Add the parsley and
  chives; mix and set aside.
— To prepare the vinaigrette,
  whip the vinegar with a
  whisk while adding the
  lemon juice, honey and
  mustard.
— Whipping constantly, add
  the oil in a thin stream.
— Pour the vinaigrette over
  the greens just before
  serving.

Beets Julienne

Ingredients
8 beets
125 mL (1/2 cup) water
15 mL (1 tablespoon) vinegar
30 mL (2 tablespoons) oil
salt and pepper to taste
15 mL (1 tablespoon) butter
15 mL (1 tablespoon) flour
15 mL (1 tablespoon) lemon
juice
125 mL (1/2 cup) sour cream

Method
— Wash and quarter the
  beets and put in a dish.
— Add the water, cover and
  cook at 100% for 8 to 10
  minutes, stirring twice
  during the cooking time.
— Peel the beets and cut into
  thin strips; set aside.
— Combine the vinegar, oil,
  salt and pepper in a small
  bowl; pour over the beets
  and set aside.
— Put the butter in a dish and
  place in the microwave to
  melt at 100% for 30
  seconds.
— Stir the flour into the
  butter; add the lemon
  juice and mix well.
— Add to the beets and stir.
— Cook at 100% for 1 to 2
  minutes, stirring twice.
— Add the sour cream and
  mix well.

Broccoli and Cheese Casserole

Ingredients
1 284 g (10 oz) package frozen
broccoli, chopped
500 mL (2 cups) orange
cheddar cheese, grated
6 slices of bread, cubed
6 eggs
15 mL (1 tablespoon) flour
375 mL (1-1/2 cups) milk
5 mL (1 teaspoon) oregano
salt and pepper to taste

Method
— Place the broccoli in a
  dish, cover and cook at
  100% for 4 to 5 minutes.
— Drain and set aside.
— Place the bread cubes in a
  22.5 cm (9 in) circular
  mold; add the broccoli
  and set aside.
— Combine the eggs and
  flour in a bowl; add the
  milk and seasoning and
  pour over the broccoli.
— Add the grated cheddar
  cheese, cover and set aside
  for 1 hour.
— Uncover and set the mold
  on a raised rack in the
  oven.
— Cook at 50% for 16 to 20
  minutes, giving the dish a
  half-turn midway through
  the cooking time.
— Cover and allow to stand
  for 5 minutes.

Grapefruit with Rum

Ingredients
5 pink grapefruit
75 mL (5 tablespoons) butter
75 mL (5 tablespoons) maple sugar

75 mL (5 tablespoons) dark rum

Method
— Cut each grapefruit in half and arrange the halves on a microwave-safe platter.
— Sprinkle 7 mL (1-1/2 teaspoons) of each of the butter, maple sugar and rum over each half.
— Leaving uncovered, cook for 3 to 4 minutes at 70%, giving the platter a half-turn midway through the cooking time.
— Allow to stand for 2 minutes before serving.

Level of Difficulty	🍴
Preparation Time	20 min
Cost per Serving	$ $
Number of Servings	10
Nutritional Value	150 calories 21.5 g carbohydrate 51 I.U. Vitamin C
Food Exchanges	1 fruit exchange 1-1/2 fat exchanges
Cooking Time	4 min
Standing Time	2 min
Power Level	70%
Write Your Cooking Time Here	

Maple Ham

Level of Difficulty	🍴
Preparation Time	10 min
Cost per Serving	$
Number of Servings	10
Nutritional Value	576 calories 45 g protein 20.8 g carbohydrate
Food Exchanges	7 oz meat 1 fruit exchange
Cooking Time	1 h 30 min
Standing Time	None
Power Level	50%
Write Your Cooking Time Here	

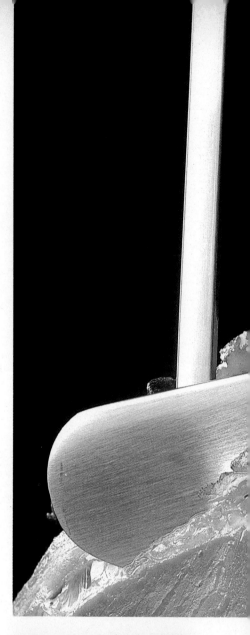

Ingredients
1 ham, 2.7 kg (6 lb)
whole cloves
250 mL (1 cup) maple syrup

Method
— Stud the ham with cloves and place in a dish.
— Pour the maple syrup over the ham and cover.
— Cook for 40 minutes at 50%.
— Turn the ham over, cover and continue cooking at 50% for 40 to 50 minutes, basting occasionally.
— Let the ham cool.

These few ingredients are all you need to prepare this wonderfully tasty ham.

MICROTIPS

Stud the ham with cloves to give it a special tang.

To Cook and Glaze a Ham Steak

Certainly, when preparing a meal for several people, it is most efficient to cook a large cut of ham, whole. A slice of ham for one or two can, however, be glazed and cooked very successfully in the microwave.

Cooking

When cooking a slice of ham, cut through the edge in two or three places. This will prevent the ham from curling up as it cooks.

Glazing

Begin by preparing your favorite glaze and put it in the microwave at 100% for 1-1/2 to 2 minutes. Put the slice of ham in a dish and pour the hot glaze over it. Cook uncovered at 50% for 7 to 10 minutes. The ham will look wonderfully appetizing —and taste as good as it looks!

Chicken and Leek Pie

Level of Difficulty	🍴🍴
Preparation Time	30 min
Cost per Serving	$
Number of Servings	10
Nutritional Value	458 calories 30.6 g protein 2.4 mg iron
Food Exchanges	4 oz meat 1 vegetable exchange 1 bread exchange 1 fat exchange
Cooking Time	1 h 53 min
Standing Time	2 min
Power Level	100%, 70%
Write Your Cooking Time Here	

Ingredients
1 chicken, 2.7 kg (6 lb)
750 mL (3 cups) boiling water
2 onions, quartered
2 carrots, sliced
1 stalk celery with leaves
1 bay leaf
5 mL (1 teaspoon) thyme
5 potatoes, cubed
5 leeks, sliced
50 mL (1/4 cup) water
50 mL (1/4 cup) butter
50 mL (1/4 cup) flour
2 egg yolks
salt and pepper to taste
2 pie shells, cooked
10 small squares of cooked pie pastry

Method
— Put the water, chicken, onion, carrots, celery, bay leaf and thyme in a large dish; cover and cook at 100% for 1 to 1-1/2 hours, or until the meat is cooked.
— Remove the chicken, bone it and cut the larger pieces into cubes; set aside.
— Strain the broth after skimming off the fat; set aside.
— Place the potatoes and leeks in a dish and add the 50 mL (1/4 cup) water; cover and cook at 100% for 6 to 8 minutes, stirring midway through the cooking time.
— Drain and set aside.
— Melt the butter at 100% for 1 minute; add the flour and stir well.
— Pour in the chicken broth and beat with a wire whisk.
— Cook at 100% for 3 to 4 minutes, stirring twice during the cooking time.
— Beat the egg yolks and add

50 mL (1/4 cup) of the hot sauce.
— Pour the egg mixture into the sauce and season.
— Divide the chicken and vegetables between the 2 shells.
— Pour the sauce over the chicken and vegetables and arrange the squares of cooked pie pastry on top.
— Heat one pie at a time for 4 to 5 minutes at 70%.
— Allow to stand for 2 minutes.

MICROTIPS

How to Clean Leeks

It can be quite difficult to get rid of all the dirt that works its way between the layers of a leek. Providing there is no need for perfect rounds, the following method may be used to simplify cleaning:

1. Place the whole leek on a cutting board.

2. With the tip of a knife, pierce the leek about 2 cm (3/4 in) from the root.

3. From this point, slit the leek lengthwise through the middle.

4. Turn the leek over and repeat. The leek will now be quite easy to clean under running water and can then be cut up as desired.

SUGGESTIONS

Maple Pie

Ingredients
250 mL (1 cup) maple syrup
250 mL (1 cup) milk
30 mL (2 tablespoons) butter
45 mL (3 tablespoons) cornstarch
50 mL (1/4 cup) cold water
2 egg yolks, beaten
5 mL (1 teaspoon) vanilla
whipped cream to garnish
chopped walnuts to garnish
1 22.5 cm (9 in) pie shell, cooked

Method
— Combine the maple syrup, milk and butter in a bowl; cook for 3 minutes at 100%.
— Dissolve the cornstarch in the cold water; add the beaten egg yolks and the vanilla.
— Add the cornstarch mixture to the hot syrup, beating constantly.
— Cook at 100% for 6 minutes, stirring vigorously every two minutes; do not allow the mixture to boil.
— Allow the mixture to stand for 15 minutes and then pour into the pie shell.
— Garnish with whipped cream and walnuts before serving.

Hot Cider

Ingredients
2 L (8 cups) cider
1 cinnamon stick
peel of 1 apple
2 cloves
nutmeg to taste

Method
— Combine all the ingredients in a deep dish.
— Cover and cook at 100% for 10 to 11 minutes, being careful not to let the mixture boil.
— Allow to stand for 15 minutes.
— Remove the cinnamon, apple peel and cloves and serve immediately.

Date Squares

Ingredients
565 g (1-1/4 lb) dates, pitted
250 mL (1 cup) crushed pineapple, with juice
250 mL (1 cup) butter or margarine
250 mL (1 cup) brown sugar, packed
375 mL (1-1/2 cups) all purpose flour
1 mL (1/4 teaspoon) salt
375 mL (1-1/2 cups) rolled oats

Method
— To prepare the date mixture, chop the dates, add the pineapple and juice, and cook at 100% for 4 minutes. Use a blender to purée and set aside.
— To prepare the cake, begin by beating the butter and sugar until creamy. Add the other ingredients and mix thoroughly.
— Pour half the cake batter into a dish and spread out evenly. Spread on the date mixture and cover with the rest of the batter.
— Cook on a rack at 70% for 10 minutes, giving the dish a half-turn midway through the cooking time.

Orange Charlotte

Ingredients
250 mL (1 cup) orange juice
1 envelope unflavored gelatin
125 mL (1/2 cup) water
125 mL (1/2 cup) sugar
15 mL (1 tablespoon) zest of

orange, grated
250 mL (1 cup) 35% cream
2 egg whites
12 lady fingers
1 orange, divided into
segments

Level of Difficulty	🍴🍴
Preparation Time	20 min*
Cost per Serving	$
Number of Servings	10
Nutritional Value	190 calories 25.9 g carbohydrate 8.6 g lipids
Food Exchanges	1 fruit exchange 1/2 bread exchange 1-1/2 fat exchanges
Cooking Time	3 min
Standing Time	None
Power Level	100%
Write Your Cooking Time Here	

Method
— Sprinkle the gelatin over the surface of the orange juice and leave for 5 minutes.
— Add the sugar to the water and cook at 100% for 2 to 3 minutes, stirring once.
— Pour the gelatin and orange juice into the hot syrup and stir.
— Add the orange zest and refrigerate until the mixture begins to set.
— Whip the cream and beat the egg whites until stiff.
— Whip the gelatin mixture and add the whipped cream and beaten egg whites.
— Arrange the lady fingers around the edge of a circular mold, alternating with the orange segments.
— Carefully spoon the orange gelatin mixture into the mold.
— Cover with waxed paper and refrigerate for 6 to 10 hours.

* The charlotte must be refrigerated for 6 to 8 hours before serving.

Mother's Day Brunch

Our message here is for husbands and children. The lot of a mother in this day and age is often not an entirely enviable one. Most mothers today hold down a job outside the home and at the same time remain responsible for the vast majority of household and child care tasks. By the time they have met all the demands placed upon them, they have very few hours left for rest and relaxation.

Does the mother in your house not deserve a real break—at least on the one day in the year that is especially set aside for her?

The brunch we are suggesting here was specifically designed for Mother's Day, but there is nothing whatsoever to stop you from preparing it at some other time of year—or indeed several times a year. It begins with two delicious salads, to be followed by egg ramekins and a savory pork spread. For your main course, a vegetable quiche and garlic chicken are sure to be a big hit, as are the date and bran muffins and the fruit salad we suggest for dessert. A tomato cocktail and chocolate madrilène add a delightful finishing touch.

The day before the brunch:
—Cook the vegetable quiche.
90 minutes before the brunch:
—Cook the garlic chicken.
20 minutes before the brunch:
—Prepare the egg ramekins; arrange the fruit salad in the parfait glasses.
10 minutes before the brunch:
—Reheat the vegetable quiche at 70% for 5 to 8 minutes.

SUGGESTIONS

Country Salad

Ingredients
1 bunch celery, diced
125 mL (1/2 cup) black olives, pitted and halved
125 mL (1/2 cup) green olives, pitted and halved
8 green onions, thinly sliced
250 mL (1 cup) green peas, cooked
250 mL (1 cup) green beans, cooked and cut julienne
750 mL (3 cups) cooked rice, cold
hard-boiled eggs, quartered, to garnish

Vinaigrette:
375 mL (1-1/2 cups) oil
125 mL (1/2 cup) cider vinegar
15 mL (1 tablespoon) salt
5 mL (1 teaspoon) pepper
15 mL (1 tablespoon) mustard powder
2 mL (1/2 teaspoon) sugar
2 mL (1/2 teaspoon) tarragon

Method
— Place all the vegetables in a salad bowl and mix; stir in the rice.
— Combine all the vinaigrette ingredients in a bowl, mix well and pour over the salad.
— Refrigerate for 1 hour and garnish with the hard-boiled egg quarters before serving.

Tomato Salad

Ingredients
8 tomatoes
salt and pepper to taste
125 mL (1/2 cup) prepared vinaigrette
50 mL (1/4 cup) fresh parsley, chopped

Method
— Cut the tomatoes in thin slices and arrange them on a serving platter so that the slices overlap; add salt and pepper to taste.
— Pour the vinaigrette over the tomato slices and sprinkle with the parsley.

Pork Spread

Ingredients
450 g (1 lb) ground pork
125 mL (1/2 cup) cracker crumbs
1 onion, grated
250 mL (1 cup) milk
salt and pepper to taste
cloves to taste
ginger to taste

Method
— Combine all the ingredients in a dish and mix well to obtain an even consistency.
— Cook for 15 minutes at 100%, stirring every 5 minutes.
— Transfer the cooked mixture to ramekin dishes and refrigerate before serving.

Egg Ramekins

Ingredients
10 eggs
10 slices bacon
160 mL (2/3 cup) mushrooms, thinly sliced
salt and pepper to taste
150 mL (2/3 cup) 35% cream
parsley, chopped
10 greased ramekin dishes

Method
— Arrange the bacon slices on a rack and cover with paper towel to prevent spattering; cook at 100% for 8 to 10 minutes.
— Crumble the cooked bacon.
— Put the sliced mushrooms in a dish; cover and cook for 3 minutes at 100%.
— Put an equal amount of mushrooms and bacon into each of the 10 ramekin dishes; break an egg into each dish and add salt and pepper to taste.
— Pour 15 mL (1 tablespoon) of cream into each dish and sprinkle with parsley.
— Place 5 of the ramekins on a raised rack and cook at 70% for 2 to 4 minutes, giving the dishes a half-turn midway through the cooking time. Repeat with the other 5 ramekins.
— Allow to stand for 2 minutes.

Level of Difficulty	🍴🍽
Preparation Time	20 min
Cost per Serving	$
Number of Servings	10
Nutritional Value	176 calories 8.7 g protein 1.5 mg iron
Food Exchanges	1 oz meat 2 fat exchanges
Cooking Time	21 min
Standing Time	2 min
Power Level	100%, 70%
Write Your Cooking Time Here	

Vegetable Quiche

Level of Difficulty	
Preparation Time	20 min
Cost per Serving	$
Number of Servings	10
Nutritional Value	265 calories 16.8 g protein 265 mg calcium
Food Exchanges	2.5 oz meat 1 vegetable exchange 1 fat exchange
Cooking Time	24 min
Standing Time	5 min
Power Level	100%, 70%
Write Your Cooking Time Here	

Ingredients
1 zucchini, sliced
12 mushrooms, sliced
175 mL (3/4 cup) green pepper, cut in strips
125 mL (1/2 cup) red pepper, cut in strips
50 mL (1/4 cup) butter
115 g (4 oz) Black Forest ham, coarsely chopped
450 g (1 lb) cooked spinach, drained and chopped
4 eggs, beaten
37 mL (2-1/2 tablespoons) flour
125 mL (1/2 cup) 18% cream
15 mL (1 tablespoon) oil
10 mL (2 teaspoons) dill, chopped
salt and pepper to taste
175 mL (3/4 cup) cheddar cheese, grated
250 mL (1 cup) mozzarella cheese, grated
paprika to taste

Method
— In a 2 L (8 cup) dish, combine the zucchini, mushrooms, peppers and butter; cover and cook at 100% for 5 to 7 minutes, stirring once midway through the cooking time.
— Add the ham and spinach, cover, and set aside.
— In another bowl, mix the beaten eggs, flour, cream, oil, dill, salt, pepper and cheddar cheese.
— Pour this mixture over the vegetables and ham and cover with the mozzarella.
— Sprinkle with the paprika.
— Place the dish on a raised rack in the oven and cook at 70% for 15 to 17 minutes, giving the dish a half-turn midway through the cooking time.
— Allow to stand 5 minutes.

To save time and effort, begin by assembling all the ingredients you need to prepare this recipe.

In a 2 L (8 cup) dish, combine the zucchini, mushrooms, peppers and butter; cover and cook at 100% for 5 to 7 minutes, stirring once.

Add the ham and spinach, cover and set aside.

Garlic Chicken

Level of Difficulty	🍴
Preparation Time	30 min
Cost per Serving	$ $
Number of Servings	10
Nutritional Value	260 calories 28.4 g protein 13.3 g lipids
Food Exchanges	3 oz meat 2-1/2 fat exchanges
Cooking Time	50 min
Standing Time	5 min
Power Level	100%, 70%
Write Your Cooking Time Here	

Ingredients
5 whole chicken breasts, split and skinned
50 mL (1/4 cup) butter
50 mL (1/4 cup) oil
5 cloves garlic, crushed
50 mL (1/4 cup) fresh parsley, chopped
175 mL (3/4 cup) white wine
175 mL (3/4 cup) chicken broth
30 mL (2 tablespoons) cornstarch
250 mL (1 cup) milk
salt and pepper to taste

Method
— Preheat a browning dish at 100% for 7 minutes, add 30 mL (2 tablespoons) of butter and 30 mL (2 tablespoons) of oil, and heat at 100% for 30 seconds.
— Brown 5 of the half-breasts; remove them and arrange in a casserole dish; set aside.
— Reheat the browning dish at 100% for 7 minutes; add the rest of the butter and oil and brown the remaining chicken breasts; add them to those in the casserole and set aside.
— Put the garlic and parsley into the browning dish.
— Add the wine and broth and cook for 3 to 4 minutes at 100%.
— Blend the cornstarch into the milk and add to the hot broth; stir.
— Cook for 3 to 4 minutes at 100%, stirring twice

during the cooking time.
— Add the seasoning and
  pour the sauce over the
  chicken breasts.
— Cover and cook at 70%
  for 37 to 42 minutes; stir
  the sauce and rearrange
  the chicken pieces twice
  during the cooking,
  moving those in the center
  to the edges of the dish.
— Allow to stand for 5
  minutes before serving.

*These are the ingredients you
will need to prepare this
succulent dish.*

MICROTIPS

To Peel and Crush
Garlic with a Knife

Choose a wide-bladed
chef's knife. Run hot
water over the clove of
garlic to make it easier to
peel. After peeling it,
place it on the cutting
board, cover it with the
flat of the knife blade
and give it a fairly firm
blow with the side of
your fist to crush it.

Date and Bran Muffins*

Ingredients
125 mL (1/2 cup) dates, coarsely chopped
250 mL (1 cup) all-bran cereal
250 mL (1 cup) milk
250 mL (1 cup) whole wheat flour
5 mL (1 teaspoon) baking powder
2 mL (1/2 teaspoon) salt
50 mL (1/4 cup) butter
125 mL (1/2 cup) brown sugar
1 egg
75 mL (1/3 cup) nuts, chopped

* This recipe makes 12 muffins.

Method
— Pour the milk into a bowl and add the cereal; set aside.
— Sift the flour with the baking powder and salt; set aside.
— Put the butter in a large dish and heat for 45 seconds at 100% to melt; add the brown sugar, the egg, the milk and cereal mixture, the sifted flour and the dates and nuts.
— Mix well and pour half the mixture into a microwave-safe, 6-muffin pan lined with paper muffin cups (large size); the cups should be no more than two-thirds full.
— Place the pan on a raised rack in the oven and cook for 2 to 2-1/2 minutes at 90%, giving the pan a half-turn midway through the cooking time.
— Unmold the muffins and allow to stand for 3 minutes.
— Repeat the 3 preceding steps with the rest of the batter.

Tomato Cocktail

Ingredients
6 tomatoes, quartered
5 mL (1 teaspoon) salt
2 mL (1/2 teaspoon) sugar
5 mL (1 teaspoon) lemon juice
Worcestershire sauce to taste
Tabasco sauce to taste
4 ice cubes
175 mL (3/4 cup) tomato juice
1 stalk celery

Method
— Combine the tomatoes, salt, sugar, lemon juice, Worcestershire sauce, Tabasco and ice cubes in a blender; mix for a few seconds until puréed.
— Strain the mixture and add the tomato juice.
— Garnish with a stalk of celery before serving.

Chocolate Madrilène

Ingredients
115 g (4 oz) semi-sweet chocolate
5 mL (1 teaspoon) butter or margarine
5 mL (1 teaspoon) cornstarch
pinch cinnamon
250 mL (1 cup) milk

Method
— Put the chocolate and the butter or margarine in a dish and heat at 50% for 30 to 45 seconds or until melted.
— Add the cornstarch and cinnamon and mix thoroughly.
— Add the milk and mix well.
— Heat for 1 minute at 70% and serve.

Fruit Salad

Ingredients
1.25 L (5 cups) fresh fruit
125 mL (1/2 cup) sour cream
10 mL (2 teaspoons) almond
extract

50 mL (1/4 cup) sugar
150 mL (2/3 cup) dried fruit

Method
— Distribute the fresh fruit
  evenly into 10 parfait
  glasses.
— Mix the sour cream,
  almond extract and sugar.
— Pour over the fresh fruit
  and garnish with the dried
  fruit.

Level of Difficulty	![icon]
Preparation Time	10 min
Cost per Serving	$
Number of Servings	10
Nutritional Value	96 calories 21.2 g carbohydrate 1.5 g lipids
Food Exchanges	1 fruit exchange 1/2 fat exchange
Cooking Time	None
Standing Time	None
Power Level	None
Write Your Cooking Time Here	

A Picnic Brunch

Summer is short—too short for us to want to miss any opportunity to enjoy the pleasures it offers.

Among the most agreeable of these pleasures has to be the possibility of gathering family and friends for a picnic brunch. All you need to do is choose a pleasant spot and prepare, ahead of time, a few dishes that can be served cold. The morning sun, a gentle breeze and the relaxed mood of your guests will do the rest.

We suggest that you begin your outdoor brunch with an Italian-style tomato salad and a potato salad with shrimps. A cold pear and watercress soup makes a refreshing follow-up. As main dishes, your guests are sure to appreciate slices of roast beef with mustard sauce and a pork and veal terrine. Bran muffins and iced melons make a delightful dessert, while fruit punch and mint tea add the perfect finishing touch.

3 days before the brunch:
—Prepare the mustard sauce to accompany the roast beef.
The day before the brunch:
—Prepare the terrine, the iced melons and the pear and watercress soup.
2 hours before the brunch:
—Take the roast out of the refrigerator so that it reaches room temperature.
1 hour before the brunch:
—Cook the roast.

Potato Salad with Shrimps

Ingredients
6 potatoes, whole and unpeeled
225 g (8 oz) shrimps, cooked and shelled
50 mL (1/4 cup) water
1 onion, finely chopped
15 mL (1 tablespoon) chives, chopped
3 dill pickles, chopped
125 mL (1/2 cup) fresh parsley, chopped
lettuce leaves

Vinaigrette:
175 mL (3/4 cup) olive oil
50 mL (1/4 cup) wine vinegar
1 clove garlic, crushed
10 mL (2 teaspoons) lemon juice
2 mL (1/2 teaspoon) rosemary
salt and pepper to taste

Garnish:
unshelled shrimps
green olives

Method
— Put the potatoes in a dish and add the water; cover and cook at 100% for 7 to 9 minutes, stirring midway through the cooking time.
— Remove the potatoes and spread them out on paper towel; leave to cool.
— Peel the potatoes and cut into cubes.
— Combine the potato cubes, onion, chives, pickles and parsley in a bowl; mix well and set aside.
— To prepare the vinaigrette, combine the oil, vinegar, garlic, lemon juice and rosemary in a bowl; add salt and pepper to taste and mix well.
— Pour half the vinaigrette over the potato mixture; cover and let stand for 1 hour at room temperature.
— Place the shelled shrimps in another bowl and add the remaining vinaigrette; cover and let stand for 1 hour at room temperature.
— Combine the shrimp and potato mixtures and refrigerate for 30 minutes.
— Arrange lettuce leaves in the bottom of a salad bowl and pour the salad onto them.
— Garnish with the unshelled shrimps and the olives before serving.

Tomato Salad Italian Style

Ingredients
5 ripe tomatoes
450 g (1 lb) mozzarella cheese
175 mL (3/4 cup) fresh basil, chopped
12 black olives
125 mL (1/2 cup) olive oil
45 mL (3 tablespoons) red wine vinegar
salt and pepper to taste

Method
— Rinse the tomatoes and cut into thin slices.
— Cut the mozzarella into thin slices.
— On a serving platter, alternate layers of tomato and mozzarella slices.
— Sprinkle the chopped basil over the top and garnish with the olives.
— Combine the oil, vinegar, salt and pepper in a bowl and pour over the tomatoes and cheese.

Pear and Watercress Soup

Ingredients
8 pears, very ripe
2 bunches watercress, leaves
and stems, chopped
1 L (4 cups) chicken stock

125 mL (1/2 cup) 35% cream
30 mL (2 tablespoons) lemon
juice
salt and pepper to taste

Method
— Peel and core the pears,
  reserving the cores and
  peelings.
— Put half the chicken
  stock in a bowl; cut the
  pears into quarters,
  immersing them in the
  stock to prevent them
  from discoloring. Set
  aside.
— Put the remaining stock
  in another bowl and add
  the cores and peelings;
  cover and cook at 100%
  for 8 to 10 minutes to
  extract maximum flavor
  and then strain.
— Add the watercress to the
  strained broth; cover and
  cook at 100% for 8 to 10
  minutes.
— Add the pear quarters
  and their stock to the hot
  broth and purée in a
  blender.
— Add the cream and lemon
  juice and season to taste.
— Refrigerate for a few
  hours before serving.

Level of Difficulty	
Preparation Time	20 min*
Cost per Serving	$
Number of Servings	10
Nutritional Value	120 calories 9.4 g carbohydrate 3.7 g lipids
Food Exchanges	1 fruit exchange 1 fat exchange
Cooking Time	20 min
Standing Time	None
Power Level	100%
Write Your Cooking Time Here	

* The soup must be refrigerated before serving.

Roast Beef with Mustard Sauce

Level of Difficulty	🍴
Preparation Time	20 min*
Cost per Serving	$ $
Number of Servings	10
Nutritional Value	480 calories 62.4 g protein 5.2 mg iron
Food Exchanges	6.5 oz meat 1 fat exchange
Cooking Time	5 min + 11 to 17 min/kg (5 to 8 min/lb)
Standing Time	10 min
Power Level	100%, 70%
Write Your Cooking Time Here	🍎✏️

* Prepare the sauce a few days ahead.

Ingredients

1 eye of round roast, 2.7 kg (6 lb)
50 mL (1/4 cup) butter, softened
10 mL (2 teaspoons) sugar
15 mL 1 tablespoon) mustard powder
2 cloves garlic, sliced
2 bay leaves

Sauce:
125 mL (1/2 cup) mustard powder
30 mL (2 tablespoons) cider vinegar
125 mL (1/2 cup) boiling water
90 mL (6 tablespoons) sugar
5 mL (1 teaspoon) salt

Method

— To make the sauce, combine the vinegar and the boiling water; stir in the mustard powder, sugar and salt.
— Cook at 100% for 5 minutes or until the sauce is smooth and slightly syrupy, stirring every minute.
— Allow to cool and store at room temperature for a few days.
— To prepare the roast beef, mix the butter, sugar and mustard powder and brush over the meat.
— Make small slits in the roast and insert garlic slices; place the roast on a rack in a baking dish and add the bay leaves.
— Cook at 70% to your liking:
very rare: 11 min/kg (5 min/lb);
rare: 13 min/kg (6 min/lb);
medium: 15 min/kg (7 min/lb);
well done: 17 min/kg (8 min/lb);
or, using a temperature probe:
very rare: 39°C (100°F);
rare: 44°C (110°F);
medium: 49°C (120°F);

well done: 60°C (140°F).
— Cover the roast with
  aluminum foil and allow
  to stand for 10 minutes.

*These are the ingredients you
will need to prepare this recipe.*

*Stir the sauce every minute
during the cooking time.*

Veal and Pork Terrine with Cognac

Level of Difficulty	🍴
Preparation Time	20 min*
Cost per Serving	$ $
Number of Servings	10
Nutritional Value	244 calories 14.8 g protein 21.3 g lipids
Food Exchanges	2 oz meat 2 fat exchanges
Cooking Time	23 min
Standing Time	None
Power Level	100%, 70%
Write Your Cooking Time Here	

* The terrine must be chilled before serving.

Ingredients
225 g (8 oz) ground veal
225 g (8 oz) veal liver, chopped
225 g (8 oz) ground pork
115 g (4 oz) pork fat, chopped
1 egg
30 mL (2 tablespoons) 35% cream
2 cloves garlic, chopped
1 onion, grated
1 mL (1/4 teaspoon) thyme
1 mL (1/4 teaspoon) chervil
45 mL (3 tablespoons) cognac
salt and pepper to taste
225 g (8 oz) bacon
1 bay leaf

Method
— Combine the veal, veal liver, pork, pork fat, egg, cream and garlic in a bowl; mix well and set aside.
— Put the onion in a dish, cover and cook at 100% for 1 minute.
— Add the onion to the meat mixture along with the thyme, chervil and cognac.
— Add salt and pepper to taste and mix well.
— Line the bottom and sides of a bowl with the bacon slices, leaving enough hanging over the edges to fold back over the top.
— Put the meat mixture into the bowl and garnish with a bay leaf.
— Fold the overhanging bacon slices back over the meat mixture.
— Cook uncovered at 100% for 5 minutes.
— Remove the liquid that has seeped out.
— Reduce the power to 70% and continue to cook for 13 to 17 minutes, once again draining off any liquid and giving the dish a half-turn midway through the cooking time.
— If necessary, drain off any liquid again when cooking is complete and allow to cool completely and refrigerate before serving.

MICROTIPS

To Make Your Own Croutons and Breadcrumbs

For croutons, use whole wheat or multi-grain bread if at all possible. Slice the bread if necessary and toast the slices in the toaster. Cut the toasted slices into small cubes, and either leave them to dry at room temperature for a few hours or put them very briefly in the microwave. For extra flavor, spread a bit of garlic butter over the warm slices of toasted bread before cutting them.

To make breadcrumbs, leave leftover odds and ends of bread to dry out completely or dry them out in the microwave oven. Pulverize the dried bread in a blender. Breadcrumbs can be flavored by adding dried herbs.

Line the bottom and sides of the bowl with the bacon slices, leaving enough hanging over to fold back over the top of the meat mixture.

75

SUGGESTIONS

Bran Muffins with Molasses*

Ingredients
375 mL (1-1/2 cups) bran
50 mL (1/4 cup) molasses
5 mL (1 teaspoon) margarine, melted
375 mL (1-1/2 cups) skim milk
1 egg
250 mL (1 cup) flour
5 mL (1 teaspoon) salt
10 mL (2 teaspoons) baking powder

Method
— Place 6 large paper muffin cups in an appropriate microwave-safe muffin pan.
— Combine the molasses, margarine, milk, egg and bran; set aside.
— In another bowl, sift the flour, salt and baking powder.
— Add the dry ingredients to the first mixture and combine thoroughly.
— Pour half the batter into the muffin cups; they should be no more than two-thirds full.
— Place the muffin pan on a raised rack in the microwave and cook at 90% for 2-1/2 to 3 minutes, giving the dish a half-turn midway through the cooking time.
— Turn the muffins out and allow to stand for 3 minutes.
— Cook the remaining 6 muffins in the same way.

* This recipe makes 12 muffins.

Festive Fruit Punch

Ingredients
1 small pineapple, cubed
15 red grapes, halved
15 green grapes, halved
15 strawberries, halved
15 raspberries
500 mL (2 cups) brandy
500 mL (2 cups) cointreau
3 to 4 bottles very dry white wine

Method
— Place all the fruit in a bowl and add the brandy and cointreau; mix well and leave to stand overnight at room temperature.
— Remove 250 mL (1 cup) of the fruit mixture and pour into a ring mold; add enough wine to almost fill the mold.
— Put the mold in the freezer and leave it for at least 24 hours.
— Unmold the frozen ring into a large punch bowl and add the remaining fruit mixture.
— Add the rest of the white wine, stir and serve.

Mint Tea

Ingredients
2 L (8 cups) cold water
375 mL (1-1/2 cups) fresh mint or
175 mL (3/4 cup) dried mint
honey or lemon slices to taste

Method
— Put the mint in a large bowl and add the water.
— Cover and set aside for 20 to 30 minutes.
— Heat for 10 to 15 minutes at 100%.
— Allow to stand for 5 minutes.
— Serve, accompanied by honey or lemon slices—or both so that your guests can choose.

Iced Melons

Ingredients

1 honeydew melon
1 cantaloupe
1 envelope lime-flavored jello powder

1 envelope strawberry-flavored jello powder
450 g (1 lb) cream cheese
50 mL (1/4 cup) milk

Level of Difficulty	🍴🍴🍴
Preparation Time	30 min*
Cost per Serving	**$**
Number of Servings	10
Nutritional Value	255 calories 21.5 g carbohydrate 18 g lipids
Food Exchanges	1-1/2 fruit exchanges 3-1/2 fat exchanges
Cooking Time	None
Standing Time	None
Power Level	None
Write Your Cooking Time Here	

Method

— Peel the two melons.
— Cut a slice off the bottom of each melon so that it will stand.
— Cut into the top of the melons, scoop out the seeds and drain.
— Prepare the lime jello according to instructions and pour into the honeydew melon.
— Prepare the strawberry jello according to instructions and pour into the cantaloupe.
— Refrigerate the melons until the jello has set.
— Slice and serve on a bed of lettuce.
— Combine the milk and the cream cheese. (If the cheese is cold, warm it first in the microwave for 40 to 60 seconds at 30%.)
— Serve the cream cheese mixture as a garnish.

* The melons must be refrigerated until the jello has set before serving.

A Brunch
for the Younger Set

Given the number of families in which both parents hold down full-time jobs, it is no wonder that parents and children these days often feel that they have somehow lost touch with one another. We all cherish the idea that weekends at least remain "family time." In actual fact, however, it all too often happens that several family members, including—perhaps even especially—the children, are then involved in activities that scatter them in various directions.

If you are among the many parents who feel that they are seeing too little of their children, one way of remedying the situation would be to organize a brunch especially for them. It could be strictly a family occasion with the emphasis on pleasing the children or, perhaps even better, it could be one for the particular purpose of including a few of their friends. Your youngsters are sure to be delighted by the idea of hosting such an out-of-the-ordinary event, and it will provide you not only with an opportunity to do something for them but also with an opportunity to become better acquainted with their friends and to gain some insights into their activities.

With this in mind, we have prepared a brunch menu that is sure to please even the pickiest eaters among the younger set. As most children are inveterate munchers, the first course of raw vegetables and dip will likely disappear in a wink. (And it is healthy too!) So be prepared to follow it quickly with eggs on a muffin, sausages and bacon, a macaroni casserole and chicken kebabs. Even the most finicky of budding gourmets will be satisfied— and positively enchanted when you follow up with fruit kebabs and chocolate chip cake. Liberal quantities of fruit punch or hot chocolate decorated with marshmallows provide the finishing touch.

The day before the brunch:
—Prepare the macaroni casserole and refrigerate.

1 hour before the brunch:
—Remove the macaroni casserole from the refrigerator; prepare the chicken kebabs but do not cook.

40 minutes before the brunch:
—Prepare the eggs on a muffin but do not cook.

30 minutes before the brunch:
—Heat the macaroni casserole at 90% for 8 to 10 minutes, stirring twice during the cooking time.

12 minutes before the brunch:
—Cook the chicken kebabs.

5 minutes before the brunch:
—Cook the eggs on a muffin and the fruit kebabs.

SUGGESTIONS

Sausages and Bacon

Ingredients
48 mini-sausages
900 g (2 lb) bacon
8 slices processed cheese

Method
— Arrange 6 slices of bacon on a bacon rack and cook at 100% for 3 to 4 minutes, giving the rack a half-turn midway through the cooking time.
— Cook another 6 slices of bacon in the same way and repeat until all the bacon is cooked.
— Cut the bacon slices in half.
— Slit each sausage lengthwise about three-quarters of the way through; be careful not to split it completely in two.
— Cut each slice of cheese into 6 strips, for a total of 48 strips.
— Insert a strip of cheese into the slit in each sausage.
— Wrap a half-slice of bacon around each sausage and secure with a toothpick.
— Place 12 sausages in a dish and cook at 100% for 2 to 3 minutes or until the sausage is cooked, giving the dish a half-turn midway through the cooking time.
— Cook another 12 sausages in the same way and repeat until all the sausages are cooked.

Vegetables Julienne

Ingredients
2 carrots
1/2 rutabaga
2 stalks celery
10 small green onions
2 green peppers
2 red peppers
50 mL (1/4 cup) water

Method
— Wash the vegetables and cut them into narrow strips (julienne).
— Put the carrots and rutabaga in a dish and add the water.
— Cook at 100% for 4 to 6 minutes, stirring midway through the cooking time.
— Drain and leave to cool.
— Arrange the vegetables on a serving dish and serve with dips.

Dips

Ingredients
175 mL (3/4 cup) plain yoghurt
4 to 6 chives, chopped
1/2 clove garlic, chopped
30 mL (2 tablespoons) bacon, cooked and crumbled

Method
— Combine all the ingredients, chill in the refrigerator and serve.

Ingredients
225 g (8 oz) cream cheese
50 mL (1/4 cup) 10% cream
1 onion, finely chopped
15 mL (1 tablespoon) dried parsley

Method
— Combine all the ingredients and serve at room temperature.

Eggs on a Muffin

Ingredients
8 eggs
8 English muffin halves,
toasted

8 slices back bacon
8 slices cheddar cheese

Method
— Break the eggs into a bowl
  and beat with a fork.
— Cook for 5 to 6 minutes at
  100%, stirring every
  minute.
— On each muffin half, place
  one slice of bacon, one
  slice of cheese and one-
  eighth of the cooked eggs.
— Cook at 100% for 2 to 3
  minutes or until the cheese
  is melted, giving the dish a
  half-turn midway through
  the cooking time.

Level of Difficulty	(icon)
Preparation Time	10 min
Cost per Serving	$
Number of Servings	8
Nutritional Value	323 calories 22.8 g protein 280 mg calcium
Food Exchanges	3 oz meat 1 bread exchange
Cooking Time	9 min
Standing Time	None
Power Level	100%
Write Your Cooking Time Here	(icon)

Macaroni Casserole

Level of Difficulty	
Preparation Time	15 min
Cost per Serving	$
Number of Servings	10
Nutritional Value	175 calories 12.2 g protein 18.2 g carbohydrate
Food Exchanges	1 oz meat 1 vegetable exchange 1 bread exchange
Cooking Time	34 min
Standing Time	None
Power Level	100%
Write Your Cooking Time Here	

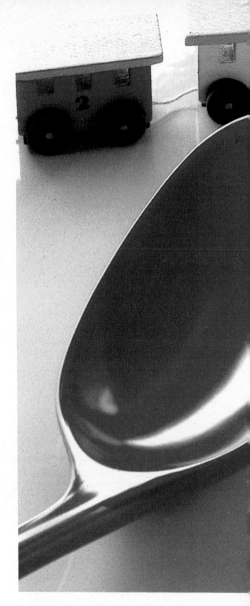

Ingredients
375 mL (1-1/2 cups) elbow macaroni
1.5 L (6 cups) water
salt to taste
5 mL (1 teaspoon) oil

Sauce:
2 small onions, finely chopped
2 stalks celery, finely chopped
450 g (1 lb) lean ground beef
1 796 mL (28 oz) can tomatoes, chopped
1 540 mL (19 oz) can tomato juice
salt and pepper to taste
50 mL (1/4 cup) cheddar cheese, grated

Method
— Add the salt and oil to the water and bring it to a boil by heating at 100% for 8 to 10 minutes.
— Add the macaroni and cook for 5 to 7 minutes at 100%, stirring twice during the cooking time.
— Drain the macaroni and rinse with cold water; set aside.
— Put the onions and celery in a dish; cover and cook at 100% for 3 to 4 minutes, stirring midway through the cooking time.

— Add the ground beef and cook at 100% for 5 to 6 minutes, interrupting the cooking twice to break up the meat with a fork.
— Add the macaroni and the rest of the ingredients to the meat; mix well.
— Cook at 100% for 5 to 7 minutes or until heated through, stirring twice during the cooking time.

To save time, begin by assembling and measuring out the ingredients you will need.

To prevent sticking, stir the macaroni twice during the cooking time.

When cooking the meat, take it out of the oven a couple of times to break it up with a fork.

83

Chicken Kebabs

Level of Difficulty	🍴
Preparation Time	20 min
Cost per Serving	$
Number of Servings	8
Nutritional Value	130 calories 14.5 g protein 9 mg iron
Food Exchanges	1.5 oz meat 1/2 vegetable exchange 1/2 fat exchange
Cooking Time	12 min
Standing Time	3 min
Power Level	70%
Write Your Cooking Time Here	

Ingredients
2 whole chicken breasts
2 green peppers, cut into pieces
2 onions, quartered
225 g (8 oz) mushrooms
2 oranges, unpeeled and quartered

Sauce:
30 mL (2 tablespoons) oil
30 mL (2 tablespoons) soy sauce
2 cloves garlic, thinly sliced
10 mL (2 teaspoons) ginger
5 mL (1 teaspoon) sugar

Method
— Combine all the sauce ingredients in a bowl and mix well.
— Skin and bone the chicken breasts and cut the meat into cubes.
— Alternate the chicken cubes and vegetables on wooden skewers, finishing at each end with a section of orange.
— Brush with the sauce.
— Place the kebabs so that they are suspended over a dish, resting the ends of the skewers on the edges of the dish.
— Cook at 70% for 8 to 12 minutes. Halfway through the cooking time, rearrange the skewers so that those in the center are toward the outside and brush with more sauce.
— Allow to stand for 3 minutes.

84

MICROTIPS

To Defrost Chicken Breasts

To ensure even defrosting of chicken breasts, use a bacon rack if possible so that the meat is never in contact with its juices. Arrange the breasts so that they are evenly spaced one from another. Divide the total defrosting time (which will depend on the total weight) into several defrosting periods interspersed with periods of standing time. Halfway through the defrosting process, rearrange the breasts so that the parts that were in the center are at the edges of the rack. After the last defrosting period remove the breasts from the oven and leave to stand for 10 minutes. This final period of standing time is necessary to allow the internal heat to spread evenly through each of the chicken breasts.

Arrange the kebabs in a dish, resting the ends of the wooden skewers on the sides of the dish.

SUGGESTIONS

Chocolate Chip Cake

Ingredients
175 g (6 oz) chocolate chips
75 mL (1/3 cup) peanut oil
2 squares unsweetened chocolate
175 mL (3/4 cup) water
250 mL (1 cup) sugar
1 egg
300 mL (1-1/4 cups) flour
2 mL (1/2 teaspoon) salt
2 mL (1/2 teaspoon) baking soda
5 mL (1 teaspoon) vanilla
75 mL (1/3 cup) nuts, chopped

Method
— Put the oil and chocolate squares in a 20 cm (8 in) square dish.
— Heat for 1-1/2 minutes at 100% and stir.
— Add all the other ingredients except the chocolate chips and the nuts.
— Beat with a fork until creamy.
— Sprinkle on the chocolate chips and the nuts.
— Cover the corners of the dish with strips of aluminum foil.
— Cook at 70% for 5 to 9 minutes, giving the dish a half-turn and removing the strips of foil halfway through the cooking time.

Stewed Peaches and Plums

Ingredients
8 peaches
10 plums
125 mL (1/2 cup) hot water
375 mL (1-1/2 cups) sugar
juice of half a lemon
zest of 1 lemon, grated

Method
— Peel the peaches and the plums, remove the stones and dice the flesh.
— Place the fruit in a dish and add the water and the sugar.
— Cover and cook at 100% for 7 to 9 minutes, stirring twice during the cooking time.
— Stir with a wooden spoon and sprinkle on the lemon juice.
— Allow to cool and garnish with the lemon zest before serving.

Fruit Punch

Ingredients
1 L (4 cups) orange juice
500 mL (2 cups) grapefruit juice
500 mL (2 cups) pineapple juice
8 cherries

Method
— Pour all the fruit juice into a large bowl and stir.
— Place the cherries in an ice-cube tray and fill with punch.
— Freeze for at least 12 hours; cover and refrigerate the remaining punch.
— Transfer the frozen cubes into the punch, stir and serve.

Hot Chocolate

Ingredients
175 mL (3/4 cup) milk
15 mL (1 tablespoon) powdered hot chocolate mix
1 large marshmallow

Method
— Combine the milk and chocolate powder in a cup.
— Heat at 90% for 1-1/2 minutes, stirring once during the cooking time.
— Garnish with the marshmallow before serving.

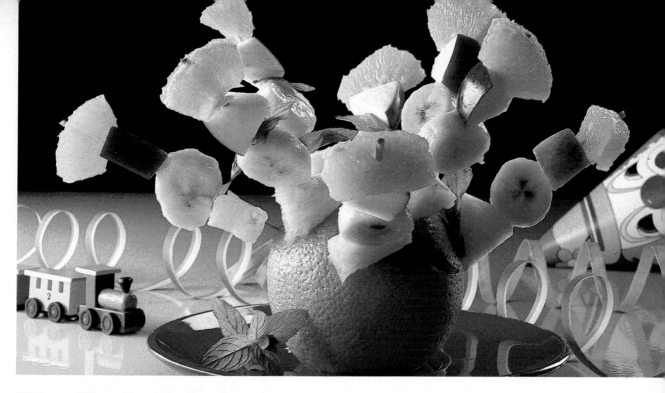

Hot Fruit Kebabs

Ingredients

250 mL (1 cup) unsweetened orange juice
15 mL (1 tablespoon) cornstarch

15 mL (1 tablespoon) water
pinch cinnamon
1 apple, cut in 2.5 cm (1 in) cubes
1 540 mL (19 oz) can

pineapple tidbits
1 540 mL (19 oz) can mandarins
1 banana, cut in 1.25 cm (1/2 in) slices

Level of Difficulty	🍴
Preparation Time	20 min
Cost per Serving	$
Number of Servings	8
Nutritional Value	59 calories 14.9 g carbohydrate 22.6 I.U. Vitamin C
Food Exchanges	1 fruit exchange
Cooking Time	5 min
Standing Time	None
Power Level	100%
Write Your Cooking Time Here	✏️

Method
— Heat the orange juice at 100% for 2 minutes.
— Dissolve the cornstarch in the water and add to the orange juice; heat at 100% for 1 minute, stirring once.
— Stir in the cinnamon.
— Alternate the pieces of fruit on 8 wooden skewers.
— Set the kebabs on a dish, the ends of the skewers resting on the sides, and brush them generously with the sauce.
— Heat at 100% for 2 minutes, turning the kebabs over midway through the cooking time.

A Friendly Get-Together

How often do you find yourself finishing off a note in a Christmas card or a telephone conversation with a friend by saying: "It's been so long . . . we really must get together soon!" If you are like most of us, all too often. We cherish our friends, we think of them frequently, but somehow the weeks and months slip by without our managing to fit a meeting into our busy schedules.

The next time you find yourself wishing you saw more of old friends, why not do something about it? Instead of waiting for some obvious occasion for a get-together, go ahead and create the occasion—invite them to a brunch. They will be glad you did and so will you!

The brunch we suggest for such a get-together is one your friends will long remember. It begins with a rice quiche, to be followed by endive and ham roll-ups with cheese sauce and salmon-stuffed potato boats. For your main course, an omelette with tomato sauce and a lobster fricassee are sure to delight your guests, as will a festive pudding for dessert. White wine and a pineapple and strawberry punch will provide the perfect finishing touch to the occasion.

The day before the brunch:
—Prepare the potato shells and the salmon filling for them; prepare the lobster fricassee but do not cook; prepare the punch.

1 hour before the brunch:
—Assemble the potato boats.

30 minutes before the brunch:
—Prepare the omelette and tomato sauce but do not cook immediately.

20 minutes before the brunch:
—Cook the lobster fricassee at 70% for 8 to 10 minutes, stirring twice during the cooking time; cover and set aside until it is time to fill the lobster shells and serve it.

10 minutes before the brunch:
—Cook the salmon-stuffed potato boats; cook the omelette.

SUGGESTIONS

Rice Quiche

Ingredients
175 mL (3/4 cup) rice
500 mL (2 cups) boiling water
8 slices bacon
1 onion, chopped
125 mL (1/2 cup) mushrooms, sliced
1 green pepper, chopped
1 tomato, chopped
15 mL (1 tablespoon) butter
4 eggs
250 mL (1 cup) 18% cream
15 mL (1 tablespoon) flour
5 mL (1 teaspoon) salt
white pepper to taste
375 mL (1-1/2 cups) mozzarella cheese, grated
paprika to garnish

Method
— Pour the boiling water into a dish and add the rice.
— Cover and cook at 100% for 5 minutes; lower the power level to 70% and cook for another 10 minutes; set aside to cool.
— Place the bacon slices on a rack and cook at 100% for 6 to 7 minutes or until it is crispy; crumble and set aside.
— Put the bacon fat into a dish and add the onion, mushrooms and green pepper.
— Cover and cook at 100% for 2 to 3 minutes, stirring once during the cooking time.
— Add the chopped tomato and mix well; set aside.
— Grease a quiche dish with the butter and spread the rice evenly over the bottom.
— Spread the crumbled bacon and cooked vegetables over the rice and set aside.
— In a bowl, beat the eggs, cream, flour, salt and pepper to a creamy consistency.
— Pour the egg mixture over the rice, bacon and vegetables; add the mozzarella and sprinkle with paprika.
— Place the quiche on a raised rack in the oven and cook at 70% for 12 to 14 minutes, giving the dish a half-turn midway through the cooking time.

Endive and Ham Roll-Ups

Ingredients
6 endives
12 slices cooked ham
water and lemon juice (for soaking the endives)
15 mL (1 tablespoon) water
15 mL (1 tablespoon) lemon juice

Cheddar Sauce:
375 mL (1-1/2 cups) cheddar cheese, grated
30 mL (2 tablespoons) butter
30 mL (2 tablespoons) flour
2 mL (1/2 teaspoon) mustard powder
250 mL (1 cup) milk
salt to taste

Method
— Cut the endives in half lengthwise and soak them for a few minutes in water to which some lemon juice has been added.
— Place the endives in a dish and pour the 15 mL (1 tablespoon) of water and the 15 mL (1 tablespoon) of lemon juice over them.
— Cover and cook at 100% for 4 minutes, or until the endives are cooked but still crunchy; drain well.
— Roll each half-endive up in a slice of ham; secure with toothpicks and set aside.
— To prepare the cheddar sauce, place the butter in a dish and heat for 45 seconds at 100%.
— Add the flour and mustard powder and mix well.
— Add the milk and cook at 100% for 2 to 3 minutes, or until thickened.
— Add the grated cheddar cheese and salt, and stir until the cheese is melted and the mixture is consistent.
— Pour the sauce over the ham roll-ups and reheat at 70% for 3 minutes before serving.

Salmon-Stuffed Potato Boats

Ingredients
8 large potatoes, cooked in
their jackets
1 213 mL (7-1/2 oz) can
salmon
30 mL (2 tablespoons) butter
50 mL (1/4 cup) onion, grated
30 mL (2 tablespoons) flour
250 mL (1 cup) milk
15 mL (1 tablespoon) parsley,
chopped
salt and pepper to taste
250 mL (1 cup) mozzarella
cheese, grated
paprika to taste

Method
— Cut the potatoes in half,
lengthwise.
— Scoop most of the pulp out
of the potato halves,
leaving a layer 0.5 cm (1/4
inch) thick lining the skin
(the removed pulp can be
saved for use at a later
date).
— Melt the butter in a dish at
100% for 30 seconds; add
the onion and cook at
100% for 1 minute.
— Add the flour and mix
well.
— Add the milk and beat

with a wire whisk.
— Cook at 100% for 3 to 4
minutes, stirring twice
during the cooking time.
— Add the salmon, parsley,
salt and pepper; mix well.
— Spoon the salmon mixture
into the potato skins and
sprinkle with the cheese
and paprika.
— Cook 8 potato boats at a
time at 100% for 2 to 3
minutes, or until the
cheese is melted, giving
the dish a half-turn
midway through the
cooking time.

Omelette with Tomato Sauce

Level of Difficulty	🍴
Preparation Time	15 min
Cost per Serving	$
Number of Servings	10
Nutritional Value	118 calories 7.2 g protein 4.5 g carbohydrate
Food Exchanges	1 oz meat 1/2 fat exchange
Cooking Time	26 min
Standing Time	2 min
Power Level	100%, 70%
Write Your Cooking Time Here	✏️

Ingredients
10 eggs
50 mL (1/4 cup) 10% cream
2 cloves garlic, finely chopped
1 small onion, finely chopped
15 mL (1 tablespoon) butter

Tomato Sauce:
375 mL (1-1/2 cups) chicken broth
175 mL (3/4 cup) tomato paste
30 mL (2 tablespoons) green onion, finely chopped
2 mL (1/2 teaspoon) chervil
7 mL (1-1/2 teaspoons) oregano
2 mL (1/2 teaspoon) crushed chili peppers
salt and pepper to taste

Method
— Combine all the sauce ingredients in a dish.
— Cook uncovered at 100% for 15 minutes, stirring every 5 minutes.
— To make the omelette, put the garlic, onion and butter in a round 25 cm (10 inch) microwave-safe dish.
— Cook at 100% for 2 minutes, stirring halfway through the cooking time.
— Beat the eggs with the cream, pour over the cooked onion and garlic, and stir.
— Cook on a raised rack in the oven at 70% for 7 to 9 minutes, stirring with a fork to transfer the mixture from the center of the dish to the edges after 4 minutes.
— Allow to stand for 2 minutes and serve with the tomato sauce.

Here are the ingredients needed to prepare this succulent omelette with tomato sauce.

Stir the tomato sauce every 5 minutes during cooking to ensure uniform consistency.

Cook the garlic and onion in the butter before adding the mixture of eggs and cream.

Lobster Fricassee

Level of Difficulty	
Preparation Time	30 min
Cost per Serving	$ $ $
Number of Servings	10
Nutritional Value	86 calories 8 g protein 4.4 g lipids
Food Exchanges	1.5 oz meat 1/2 vegetable exchange 1 fat exchange
Cooking Time	12 min
Standing Time	None
Power Level	100%, 70%
Write Your Cooking Time Here	

Ingredients
5 225 g (8 oz) lobsters, cooked
45 mL (3 tablespoons) butter
2 cloves garlic, chopped
6 green onions, thinly sliced
50 mL (1/4 cup) fresh parsley, chopped
5 mL (1 teaspoon) thyme
5 tomatoes, peeled and chopped
45 mL (3 tablespoons) tomato paste
150 mL (2/3 cup) white wine
2 mL (112 teaspoon) cayenne pepper

Method
— Split the lobsters in two and remove the meat; reserve the shells.
— Cut the lobster meat into cubes.
— Put the butter in a dish and melt at 100% for 1 minute; add the garlic and green onions and cook at 100% for 2 minutes, stirring once during the cooking time.
— Add all the remaining ingredients except the lobster and stir.
— Cook for 4 to 5 minutes at 100%.
— Stir and add the lobster meat.
— Cook for another 3 to 4 minutes at 70%, stirring once during the cooking time.
— Pour into the reserved lobster shells and serve.

MICROTIPS

Removing the Meat from a Lobster

About 30% of a lobster's weight is meat. All of it can be removed relatively easily by using the technique appropriate to each part. First, cook the lobster and set it aside on its back to cool.

The Legs
Detach the eight legs. Break each one in two at the middle joint and remove the meat by means of a lobster pick.

The Claws
Detach the claws and break open the shell to get the meat out. A mallet along with a lobster pick give excellent results.

The Trunk and Tail
With a sharp knife, cut along the membrane on either side of the abdomen. Pull it away, starting at the tail. Remove the meat in one piece.

The Liver, Gall Bladder and Coral
Finally, use a spoon to remove the liver (edible) and the gall bladder (not edible). The shell of a female lobster may contain pinkish eggs known as coral. This is edible.

SUGGESTIONS

Festive Pudding

Ingredients
2 92 g (3.25 oz) packets vanilla instant pudding mix
500 mL (2 cups) milk
500 mL (2 cups) 18% cream
10 mL (2 teaspoons) almond extract
1 L (4 cups) berries (strawberries, raspberries or blueberries)
500 mL (2 cups) 35% cream, whipped
50 mL (1/2 cup) almonds, roasted
50 mL (1/4 cup) walnuts, coarsely chopped

Method
— Prepare the instant pudding, using equal parts of milk and 18% cream.
— Add the almond extract and mix well; set aside for two minutes.
— Assemble the dessert in parfait glasses, layering the ingredients in the following order: half the pudding, half the fruit, the remaining pudding and a last layer of fruit.
— Garnish with the whipped cream and sprinkle with the almonds and walnuts just before serving.

Boston Cream Cake

Ingredients

Cake:
7 egg whites
325 mL (1-1/3 cups) sugar
7 egg yolks, beaten
75 mL (1/3 cup) oil
375 mL (1-1/2 cups) flour
15 mL (1 tablespoon) baking powder
pinch salt
5 mL (1 teaspoon) vanilla extract

Fudge Sauce:
120 mL (8 tablespoons) hot water
105 mL (3-1/2 oz) shortening
15 mL (1 tablespoon) honey
175 mL (3/4 cup) cocoa
30 mL (2 tablespoons) butter
pinch salt
875 mL (3-1/2 cups) icing sugar

Pastry cream:
See *Desserts,* Volume 3, page 100

Method
— To make the cake, beat the egg whites to stiff peaks; gradually add the sugar while beating continuously.
— Add the beaten egg yolks, oil, flour, baking powder, salt and vanilla extract; mix thoroughly.
— Pour the batter into 3 20 cm (8 in) round cake pans that have been lined with waxed paper.
— Cook one cake at a time on a raised rack at 70% for 3 to 5 minutes, giving the dish a half-turn midway through the cooking time.
— To make the fudge sauce, heat the water at 100% for 1 to 1-1/2 minutes.
— Add the shortening and honey; mix well.
— Add the cocoa, butter and salt and mix; then gradually add the icing sugar, beating until the mixture takes on a thick, even consistency.
— Assemble the dessert by covering one of the cakes with half the pastry cream, place the second cake on top and cover it with the remaining pastry cream. Finally, place the third cake on top and pour the fudge sauce over it.

Pineapple and Strawberry Punch

Ingredients
2 ripe pineapples
900 g (2 lb) fresh strawberries
500 mL (2 cups) sugar

2.5 L (10 cups) boiling water
lemon juice to taste
mint leaves to garnish

Level of Difficulty	🍴
Preparation Time	15 min
Cost per Serving	$
Number of Servings	10
Nutritional Value	226 calories 57.4 g carbohydrate 66.9 I.U. Vitamin C
Food Exchanges	1 fruit exchange
Cooking Time	14 min
Standing Time	None
Power Level	100%
Write Your Cooking Time Here	✏️🍎

Method
— Peel the pineapple and coarsely chop the pulp.
— Place the pineapple in a large bowl and sprinkle the sugar over it.
— Pour the boiling water over the pineapple, cover and cook at 100% for 12 to 14 minutes.
— Set aside, still covered, to cool at room temperature; stir from time to time.
— Add the lemon juice and strawberries to the pineapple and put through the blender.
— Put some ice cubes in a pitcher and pour in the punch.
— Garnish each glass of punch with a mint leaf before serving.

A Romantic Brunch

He loves to cook and delights in preparing little delicacies which he then sets before you with a skill and flair that never cease to astonish you. The atmosphere of grace and elegance he creates is such that the time you spend across the table from him passes as in a dream. He is truly a rare gem among men.

She loves to cook. When she invites you to a meal, every dish she sets before you is something out of the ordinary. The enchantment begins with the wonderful aromas that waft from her table and the combination of simplicity and elegance with which everything is set out. Never yet has she failed to make a meal a unique and memorable experience. She is truly a rare gem among women.

There is not really very much for us to teach the rare gems of this world. If, however, you are like so many of us and do not quite feel you can count yourself among them, we have a brunch menu to suggest that is sure to elevate you to that distinguished status in his or her eyes.

It begins with a vegetable salad, accompanied if you wish by Boston lettuce served with a tarragon vinaigrette. Next on the menu are ham mousse, rice salad and stuffed mushroom caps, to be followed by quails in wine. Chocolate fondue or a hot fruit salad makes a perfect dessert to linger over, while champagne punch followed by an espresso coffee add an exquisite final touch.

In the morning of the day before the brunch:
—Put the fruit for the punch to soak in the champagne and liqueurs.

In the evening of the day before the brunch:
—Put some of the punch to freeze as indicated in the recipe; prepare the vegetable salad; set the quails in the marinade; prepare the ham mousse.

35 minutes before the brunch:
Cook the quails.

5 minutes before the brunch:
—Finish preparing the champagne punch.

SUGGESTIONS

Boston Lettuce
with Tarragon Vinaigrette

Ingredients
1 head Boston lettuce
1 egg, hard-boiled and
chopped
250 mL (1 cup) carrots, grated
1 small stalk celery, diced
2 tomatoes, seeded and diced

Vinaigrette:
30 mL (2 tablespoons)
tarragon vinegar
10 mL (2 teaspoons) Dijon
mustard
10 mL (2 teaspoons) tarragon,
finely chopped
salt and pepper to taste
125 mL (1/2 cup) oil

Method
— Pull the lettuce leaves
  apart.
— Rinse the lettuce leaves
  and dry them well;
  arrange them on two
  plates.
— Prepare the viniagrette by
  mixing the vinegar,
  mustard and tarragon;
  add the salt and pepper
  and then gradually add
  the oil, whisking
  constantly.
— Pour the vinaigrette over
  the lettuce leaves; divide
  the remaining ingredients
  in two and sprinkle over
  the lettuce.

Rice Salad

Ingredients
250 mL (1 cup) brown rice,
cooked and cooled
1 red pepper, diced
4 green onions, thinly sliced
1/2 stalk celery, sliced
50 mL (1/4 cup) fresh parsley,
chopped
4 black olives, quartered

Dressing:
125 mL (1/2 cup) mayonnaise
45 mL (3 tablespoons)
ketchup
30 mL (2 tablespoons) brandy

Method
— To make the dressing,
  combine the mayonnaise,
  ketchup and brandy in a
  bowl; mix well and set
  aside.
— Combine all the other
  ingredients in a large
  bowl.
— Add the dressing and stir
  well to obtain an even
  mixture.

Stuffed Mushroom Caps

Ingredients
12 large mushrooms
30 mL (2 tablespoons) butter
30 mL (2 tablespoons) onion,
grated
50 mL (1/4 cup) Italian
breadcrumbs
parsley to taste

Method
— Remove the mushroom
  stems and chop them; set
  the caps aside.
— Melt the butter in a dish
  and add the onion and
  chopped mushroom
  stems.
— Cook at 100% for 1 to
  1-1/2 minutes or until the
  onion is tender.
— Add the breadcrumbs and
  parsley and mix well.
— Stuff the mushroom caps
  with the mixture and
  arrange on a plate.
— Cook for 1-1/2 to 2-1/2
  minutes at 100%.

Vegetable and Rice Salad

Ingredients

250 mL (1 cup) mushrooms, sliced

1/2 green pepper, cut into strips

1/2 red pepper, cut into strips

250 mL (1 cup) hot water

125 mL (1/2 cup) rice

45 mL (3 tablespoons) olive oil

125 mL (1/2 cup) basil leaves

30 mL (2 tablespoons) lemon juice

1 clove garlic

salt and pepper to taste

Level of Difficulty	🍴
Preparation Time	15 min*
Cost per Serving	$
Number of Servings	4
Nutritional Value	152 calories 1.8 g protein 113 g carbohydrate
Food Exchanges	1 vegetable exchange 112 bread exchange 2 fat exchanges
Cooking Time	11 min
Standing Time	5 min
Power Level	100%, 70%
Write Your Cooking Time Here	

Method

— Pour the water into a dish and add the rice.

— Cover and cook at 100% for 3 minutes.

— Lower the power level to 70% and cook for another 7 to 8 minutes.

— Allow to stand for 5 minutes.

— In another bowl, combine the olive oil, basil, lemon juice, garlic, salt and pepper; put through a food processor or blender until the basil is finely chopped.

— Pour the dressing over the rice and set aside until it is completely cooled.

— Add the mushrooms and the pepper strips; refrigerate for 3 hours.

* The salad must be refrigerated for 3 hours before serving.

Ham Mousse

Ingredients
300 mL (1-1/4 cups) ham, diced
1 envelope unflavored gelatin
175 mL (3/4 cup) chicken broth
15 mL (1 tablespoon) onion, grated
50 mL (1/4 cup) pecans, chopped
50 mL (1/4 cup) celery, finely chopped
125 mL (1/2 cup) mayonnaise
125 mL (1/2 cup) 35% cream

Method
— Sprinkle the gelatin over the broth; allow to stand for 5 minutes.
— Heat at 100% for 1 to 2 minutes, but do not allow to boil; stir to dissolve the gelatin.
— Add the onion and place in the refrigerator; leave until the mixture begins to set.
— Add the rest of the ingredients and stir.
— Chill a mold under cold water and pour the mixture into it.
— Refrigerate for 3 to 4 hours before serving.

Quails in Wine

Ingredients
4 quails
50 mL (1/4 cup) butter
30 mL (2 tablespoons) flour
125 mL (1/2 cup) white wine
5 mL (1 teaspoon) thyme

Marinade:
75 mL (1/3 cup) peanut oil
12 peppercorns
5 mL (1 teaspoon) thyme
50 mL (1/4 cup) fresh parsley,
chopped

Method
— Combine the marinade
  ingredients in a large bowl
  and stir.
— Put the quails in the
  marinade, making sure
  they are all well coated.
— Leave to marinate for 8 to
  12 hours, turning
  frequently.
— Preheat a browning dish at
  100% for 7 minutes; add
  the butter and heat at
  100% for another 30
  seconds.
— Sear the quails.
— Cook for 10 minutes at
  70%.
— Turn the quails over and
  move those in the center

to the edge of the dish.
— Cook for a further 10 to 12
  minutes at 70%.
— Remove the quails and
  cover them with
  aluminum foil; shiny side
  down.
— Add the flour to the
  cooking juices and stir
  thoroughly.
— Add the wine and thyme
  and deglaze with a
  spatula.
— Cook at 100% for 1 to 2
  minutes, stirring twice
  during the cooking time.
— Arrange the quails in a
  serving dish and pour the
  sauce over them.

Champagne Punch

Ingredients
1 bottle of champagne
1/2 pineapple, cubed
8 red grapes, halved

8 green grapes, halved
8 strawberries, halved
250 mL (1 cup) apricot brandy
250 mL (1 cup) cointreau

Method
— Combine the fruit, apricot brandy and cointreau in a large bowl; leave to soak overnight.
— Remove 250 mL (1 cup) of the mixture and pour into a ring mold.
— Add half the bottle of champagne and freeze for 24 hours.
— Unmold the frozen ring into a large punch bowl and add the rest of the liqueur and fruit mixture and the remaining champagne.

Level of Difficulty	🍴
Preparation Time	20 min*
Cost per Serving	$ $ $
Number of Servings	10
Nutritional Value	123 calories 9.6 g carbohydrate 8.5 I.U. Vitamin C
Food Exchanges	1 fruit exchange
Cooking Time	None
Standing Time	None
Power Level	None
Write Your Cooking Time Here	

* The preparation of this punch requires overnight soaking of the fruit followed by freezing for 24 hours.

SUGGESTIONS

Chocolate Fondue

Ingredients
284 g (10 oz) milk chocolate
300 mL (1-1/4 cups) 35%
cream
50 mL (1/4 cup) honey
60 g (2 oz) ground hazelnuts

Method
— Grate the chocolate into a
 dish.
— Add the other ingredients
 and mix well.
— Cook at 50% until the
 chocolate is melted,
 stirring every minute.
— Pour into a fondue pot
 and serve with fruit.

Hot Fruit Salad

Ingredients
250 mL (1 cup) fruit of your
choice
150 mL (2/3 cup) honey
75 mL (1/3 cup) orange juice
30 mL (2 tablespoons)
marmalade
30 mL (2 tablespoons) butter
10 mL (2 teaspoons) brandy

Method
— Combine the honey,
 orange juice, marmalade
 and butter in a bowl.
— Heat for 1 to 1-1/2
 minutes, being careful not
 to let the mixture reach
 the boiling point.
— Add the fruit and the
 brandy; cover and place in
 the refrigerator for 2
 hours.
— Place the fruit in 2
 microwave-safe serving
 goblets and add 45 to 60
 mL (3 to 4 tablespoons)
 sauce to each.
— Cover and cook for 2 to 3
 minutes at 90%, giving
 the goblets a half-turn
 midway through the
 cooking time.
— Allow to stand for 1
 minute before serving.

Chantilly Cream
with Almonds

Ingredients
1 egg white
30 mL (2 tablespoons) sugar
75 mL (1/3 cup) almonds
45 mL (3 tablespoons) butter
125 mL (1/2 cup) 35% cream
15 mL (1 tablespoon) crème
de cacao

Method
— Beat the egg white until
 stiff, gradually adding
 half the sugar.
— Put the almonds and
 butter in a dish and heat
 at 100% for 1 to 1-1/2
 minutes, or until the
 almonds are roasted,
 stirring once during the
 cooking time.
— Allow the almonds to cool
 then crush half of them.
— Whip the cream, adding
 the rest of the sugar.
— Add the crème de cacao
 and the crushed almonds
 to the whipped cream and
 fold into the beaten egg
 white.
— Pour into serving glasses
 and garnish with the rest
 of the almonds.

Glossary

Like all great arts, the art of cooking has developed a specialized vocabulary over the course of its long history. The terms used may designate methods of preparation or the dishes themselves. Because you will find these terms in the recipes in this volume as well as in other cook books, we have made a list of some of the more comonly used ones.

Charlotte: A dessert that consists primarily of a Bavarian cream (a rich egg custard set with gelatin, often flavored with fruit, and with whipped cream added) set in a mold lined with lady fingers.

Fricassee: Meat cut into pieces, stewed and served with a thick gravy.

Glaze: To brush a mixture over meat to give it a glossy appearance and to add flavor; also, to brush egg, milk or water and sugar on pastry to make it shiny.

Headcheese: A cold pork dish originally made with the pig's head; when prepared at home, it is now more commonly made with the feet and/or hocks.

Hollandaise: A basic sauce made with eggs and butter and flavored with lemon juice and cayenne. A number of other sauces are based on hollandaise.

Julienne: Fine strips of vegetables or meat. Julienne strips are usually about 3 mm (1/8 inch) thick and 4 to 5 cm (1-1/2 to 2 inches) long.

Mousse: A smooth light mixture that may be sweet or savory, usually made with beaten egg whites and cream, and sometimes set with gelatin.

Poach: To cook in a gently simmering liquid (water, stock, wine). Meat, fish, poultry and eggs can all be poached.

Punch: The word is thought to have developed in British colonial days from the Hindi word *panch,* meaning five, because it was originally made with five ingredients. Today it usually refers to a drink made with fruit or fruit juices, to which may be added some form of spirits or wine, soda water or other carbonated drinks and spices. Punches may be served hot or cold.

Ramekin: A small heat-proof container in which individual servings of various meat or egg dishes are cooked. The word also refers to the food cooked in such dishes as well as to meat and/or cheese tarts.

Terrine: Originally the word referred to a high-sided earthenware dish with handles in which certain meats were cooked and preserved. The meaning of the word has since been extended to cover dishes made of ovenproof china, metal, pyrex, etc., as well as the food prepared in them. This will usually be a seasoned meat mixture similar to pâté, though terrines may also be made with fish, poultry or vegetables. They are served cold as an hors d'oeuvres or as a starter.

Trifle: An English dessert that combines cake (usually sponge or pound cake), fruit, custard and whipped cream, often flavored with sherry and served in a large glass bowl.

Velouté: A basic sauce made with a butter and flour roux and light stock. A velouté is most commonly served with chicken but also makes an excellent accompaniment for fish. The word may also apply to a soup in which a blend of egg yolks and cream is added to give a smooth velvety consistency.

Vol-au-vent: A round case of puffed pastry (also known as a patty shell) served with a filling—most commonly meat, poultry or seafood in a thick sauce.

Drinks to Serve at Brunch

For many people, coffee is an absolutely essential element of the first meal of the day, whether this is taken early or late. But there is no real reason to grant coffee this kind of monopoly when you plan your brunch since there exists a wide range of alternatives appropriate to a late morning meal. A touch of the fanciful is never out of place at a brunch, so give your imagination free rein when choosing the drinks you will serve. The only rule that need apply is that whatever you decide on should be light. You can choose from among fruit and vegetable cocktails, made with or without alcohol, light wines, punches of all sorts and a whole range of flavored coffees and teas. Let's look more closely at a few of the possibilities.

Before Brunch

Guests who are invited for the first meal of the day are not likely to arrive with gargantuan appetites. The drinks served before the meal must therefore be chosen with care. Natural fruit and vegetable juices are ideal for awakening sleepy appetites. The virtues of orange and grapefruit juice are well known, as are those of tomato juice and vegetable cocktails. But why not consider some of the other, less well-known but equally appropriate, possibilities—cranberry juice, for instance, delicious hot or cold; pear or apricot nectar; or carrot, peach or melon juice?

The flavor of all these natural juices can be enhanced in a variety of ways: a stick of cinnamon, a *soupçon* of nutmeg and a clove or two in hot apple juice; a touch of garlic in carrot juice; fennel or parsley in tomato juice—the possibilities are virtually infinite.

To Accompany Brunch

Punches take pride of place at a brunch and, we would point out, may serve equally well as an aperitif and as a drink to accompany the meal. Depending on circumstances and the season, they can be served hot or chilled. Usually they combine fruit with sugar or syrup and a choice of wines, liqueurs or other alcoholic beverages, fruit juices, and/or soda water or other carbonated drinks.

While punch is a natural for special occasions, so are light wines. Champagnes or other sparkling wines add an extra touch of festivity. White wines, providing they are not too heavy, seem particularly appropriate to a brunch, but a delicate red wine can also be the perfect accompaniment to certain dishes, such as pâtés and terrines. Nor should you overlook the possibilities of cider, especially if the timing is such that it can be served hot and spicy.

After Brunch

Coffee, of course, has its role to play at the end of any meal, and your brunch need be no exception even if you wish to get away from the usual and conventional. Try one of the many variations such as Irish or Spanish coffee, or add a touch of distinction by flavoring your coffee with cinnamon, cardamom or other appropriate spices. Tea also makes a pleasant ending to a brunch, especially in summer, when iced tea with lemon or mint is wonderfully refreshing.

Whatever you choose to serve, it is also a good idea to have a bottle or two of mineral water on hand for guests who may prefer it.

Conversion Chart

**Conversion Chart for the
Main Measures Used in
Cooking**

Volume		Weight	
1 teaspoon	5 mL	2.2 lb	1 kg (1000 g)
1 tablespoon	15 mL	1.1 lb	500 g
		0.5 lb	225 g
1 quart (4 cups)	1 litre	0.25 lb	115 g
1 pint (2 cups)	500 mL		
1/2 cup	125 mL		
1/4 cup	50 mL	1 oz	30 g

**Metric Equivalents
for Cooking
Temperatures**

49°C	120°F	120°C	250°F
54°C	130°F	135°C	275°F
60°C	140°F	150°C	300°F
66°C	150°F	160°C	325°F
71°C	160°F	180°C	350°F
77°C	170°F	190°C	375°F
82°C	180°F	200°C	400°F
93°C	200°F	220°C	425°F
107°C	225°F	230°C	450°F

Readers will note that, in the recipes, we give 250 mL as the equivalent for 1 cup and 450 g as the equivalent for 1 lb and that fractions of these measurements are even less mathematically accurate. The reason for this is that mathematically accurate conversions are just not practical in cooking. Your kitchen scales are simply not accurate enough to weigh 454 g—the true equivalent of 1 lb—and it would be a waste of time to try. The conversions given in this series, therefore, necessarily represent approximate equivalents, but they will still give excellent results in the kitchen. No problems should be encountered if you adhere to either metric or imperial measurements throughout a recipe.

Index